F

This year, the Poetry Now Young Writers' Kaleidoscope competition proudly presents the best poetic contributions from over 32,000 up-and-coming writers nationwide.

Successful in continuing our aim of promoting writing and creativity in children, each regional anthology displays the inventive and original writing talents of 11-18 year old poets. Imaginative, thoughtful, often humorous, *Kaleidoscope Kent* provides a captivating insight into the issues and opinions important to today's young generation.

The task of editing inevitably proved challenging, but was nevertheless enjoyable thanks to the quality of entries received. The thought, effort and hard work put into each poem impressed and inspired us all. We hope you are as pleased as we are with the final result and that you continue to enjoy *Kaleidoscope Kent* for years to come.

KENT

Edited by Michelle Warrington

First published in Great Britain in 1999 by
POETRY NOW YOUNG WRITERS
Remus House,
Coltsfoot Drive,
Woodston,
Peterborough, PE2 9JX
Telephone (01733) 890066

HB ISBN 0 75430 421 3
SB ISBN 0 75430 422 1

CONTENTS

Invicta Grammar School

The Poems

DOLL-LIKE

You said I was doll-like.
A fine, white-boned, little
China plaything for you to play with.
I had real silky hair for you to plait
And eyes that you could poke at and no tears would fall.
You drowned your childhood in those eyes.

You loved to squeeze the puppet body and
Try to breathe life into your stuffed plaything.
But your doll did not want to play,
Nor did she want to be wrapped up
In pink tissue, swathed in cotton wool and
Newspapers and left to rot in a box.

Your doll's lips were set tightly closed -
A state of perfection for a woman.
The poor little twig of a bird was so
Pleasing, so beautiful, was so utterly yours.
But you see, she was not.
Inside her China head

The clockwork tick rattled
As time unleashed his grasp from her stiff limbs.
A deliberately mechanical action
Too basic to be considered as life.
But she could live without you, her maker.
A doll? No. A woman? Not yours.

Katherine Barton (17)
Ashford School

SLOVENIAN SNAPSHOT

The first crash of thunder,
The sound is deafening.
A streak of lightning,
Lights up the night sky.
The sun rises behind
Monstrous black clouds,
Seeming to block all forms of day out.
Sounds of rain reach my ears,
A sudden shaft of sunlight,
Gushing stream beside hotel swells.
Sunlight goes, as quickly as it came,
No shadows form on this lovely valley.
Finally, sun again.
A sudden rush for the door,
The world has come to life.
Clouds split, sun is blinding,
Steam everywhere.
Surrounded by a rising mist,
Walk through dripping woods,
Drips down my neck,
I'm sure my boots are leaking.
One after another the mountains
Lift up their dark veil to reveal
A multitude of wild flowers,
A riot of blue and pink.

No people walk these paths,
Eventually . . .
Our goal, the waterfall,
Rushing, roaring, gathering speed,
In the 90 metre drop,
Finally, we turn for home
The sky is crystal clear,
The views and outlines crisp,
Against the dark blue sky.
Temperatures soar,
The world is a happy place.

Helen Darbyshire (12)
Ashford School

THE RAGE

The wind is howling,
The rain is falling,
The sea is grey
And the waves
As high as houses.
The stones are hurting
My bare feet.

And then:

A patch of blue is visible,
The wind is carrying a gentle breeze.
A rainbow appears in the sky
And the stones turn to sand.
The blue waves are lapping at my feet
And once again the storm is over
Until another day.

Jessica Mead (12)
Ashford School

THE ISLAND

The hectic moods,
Tempers fraying,
Leaving the Island.
Wish I were staying.

It was a long holiday,
Ten years or so,
I was so happy.
So they decided to go.

Leaving the Island,
Was such a chore.
We had so much luggage,
It was really a bore.

Why couldn't we stay?
It would do no more harm.
I could convince them.
It was all down to charm.

The charm didn't work.
We brought a house here.
We packed up our stuff,
No reason to cheer.

The very last ferry ride,
With monsoon rain.
I close my eyes tight,
I can't bear the pain.

My Island,
A city so busy and fast.
But the Hong Kong I know,
Is now in the past.

Elizabeth Kaye (12)
Ashford School

TROPICAL PARADISE?

When we stepped off the plane,
It started to rain
On our Tropical Island Paradise

In our coastal town,
It was pouring it down
On our Tropical Island Paradise

When the rain stopped pouring,
It was time we were snoring
On our Tropical Island Paradise

When we hit the beach,
The wind started to screech
On our Tropical Island Paradise

When we swam in the sea,
We got cold as can be
On our Tropical Island Paradise

One week of hell,
You could hardly tell
This was:
Tropical Island Paradise

Lucinda Hill (12)
Ashford School

JUNE RAIN

I wanted you to know,
those weeks ago I almost
told you. But now, buried
behind my encumbered facade
was a plea for deliverance.

It was raining. A walk?
A puzzled look emerged from
the unusual request. Awkward
silence filled the air, displaying
the need for words.

Ultimately you spoke, but
with a sense of distraction.
I remained quiet. Constantly
thinking. Standing motionless,
looking downwards as the

rain dispersed across the
Weald, showing nature's touch
embracing the cold, biting rain,
that pierce my skin and blinded
my eyes. Then,

that was the moment I told
you, cutting your sentence
with scrambled, illogical words
that became devoured by the
rain.

As I turned to you I noticed
the compassion in your eyes.
They stood alone, amidst
the warm, refreshing rain that
trickled down your face.

The welcoming silence among
snatches of spoken comfort
brought our journey back
to the warm lights and happy
voices of, your home.

I continued on. To faded
lights and unspoken words.

Catherine Weaver (18)
Ashford School

LYING AWAKE

The green trees blow against the
window outside.
The window rattles.
I hear the pitter-patter of mouse feet
under the floorboards.
I hear mother bang and clatter the
dishes as she washes up.
I hear the mumble of voices as dad
watches TV.
I hear my brother on his computer
games.
I hear my sister snoring louder than
ever.
All these things keep me awake all
night!

Amelie Thomas (11)
Ashford School

AIRPORT

Car park, very dark,
Loud planes, smelly drains,
Board the bus, lots of fuss,
Everyone, tries to run.

Diet cokes, telling jokes,
Eating lots, spending pots,
Children screaming, rain teaming
Full rooms, men with brooms.

Very boring, lots of drawing,
Long queues, painful shoes,
Slow pace, heavy case,
I'm in shorts, weather in the minus noughts.

Mums and dads giving treats, babies sucking bottle teats,
O dear long delay, guess I'll have to wait all day!

Dominique Fraser (12)
Ashford School

KALEIDOSCOPE

As I turn its colours swirl,
it takes me into a different world.
The patterns change and show colour's real beauty,
the reflection in the mirrors make so much symmetry.
The patterns seem to form so simply,
it takes me into a different world,
as I turn its colours swirl.

Kate Hickmott (12)
Barton Court Grammar School

THE MARKET

The wind whistles against my ears,
Blocking the children's mocking sneers.
Savage dogs snapping at my feet,
The sickly smell of rotten meat.
Smelly dustbins crashing around,
The way they crash, a terrifying sound.
Autumn leaves drifting down from the trees,
The overcast sky, makes me freeze.

The fresh smell of luscious fruit,
The sound of a busker playing a flute.
It starts to rain, where is my hat?
I stumble on cobbles and trip over a cat.
The sizzling smell of cooking fish,
If only I could see, it would be a tasty dish.
'Gather around, half a pound of juicy ham,'
Where shall I go, it's a very hard life being a blind man.

Aarron Foster (11)
Barton Court Grammar School

KALEIDOSCOPE

Like a tunnel waiting for a light
The colours all different and bright
The shapes will always change
The colours are never the same
Like the Blackpool illumination
Like lines of communication
The lines twist and turn all magical
Most of the shapes are symmetrical
Like a bride's bouquet of flowers
The stems are tall like towers.

Mathew Gladdish (12)
Barton Court Grammar School

COLOURS AND SHAPES

Kaleidoscope; small tubes of colour,
Always different but never duller.
Leopard skin; stripes and spots,
Every colour plus colds and hots.
Indigo, red, green and blue,
Disco lights, traffic lights too.
Ovals, diamonds, circles and squares,
Scorpions, elephants, rabbits and hares.
Capturing colour and light, not sound,
Observe as all goes round and round.
People watch they listen they learn,
Everyone though just waits their turn.

Joe Tanzey (13)
Barton Court Grammar School

LOFT

I rummaged around in the dingy darkness,
Cobweb fingers pulling at my hair,
Inhaling dust,
Sounds of birds twittering in glee,
Eerie and cold,
A draught whipping around my ankles,
Scared in the everlasting darkness,
Balancing on filthy beams,
Imagination playing tricks on me,
Shapes staring at me.

Michael Haith (11)
Barton Court Grammar School

MY LOFT

My loft is dark and dingy,
And it's very small,
If you weren't very careful,
You would surely fall.

My loft, it smells like garbage,
And isn't very nice,
It's mouldy and it's horrible,
And I think that we have mice.

My loft it sounds like,
Squeaking bats,
There's old Christmas stuff,
Teddies and hats.

That's my loft,
So there we are,
That's all there is?
Not by far.

Gemma Foreman (11)
Barton Court Grammar School

KALEIDOSCOPE

Lots of colours flying around
Never landing on the ground
Always falling into place
Moving with such beautiful grace
The kaleidoscope like a Katherine wheel
Spinning like a squirmy eel
Wiggling, jiggling, spinning around
To make the shining colours resound.

Seb Richards (11)
Barton Court Grammar School

BUTTERFLY

Once I had my very own butterfly
so very much in love was I.
There it rested in my hand,
the most exquisite and stunning in the land.
Cherished with all my heart
never ever would I let it part.

It was all mine and mine alone
in my arms it was so at home.
I was and felt, so responsible
yet so completely comfortable.
Protection was my only duty
to care for such a beauty.

- But then one day,
it flapped its wings and flew away.
Never did I understand
why again it didn't land
in my outstretched and waiting hand.

Once I had my very own butterfly
so very much in love was I
but it's love for me was all a lie.

Caroline Gingell (16)
Barton Court Grammar School

THE BATTLE OF COLOURS

Red, gold and green,
banding together against,
blue, black and brown.

Red against blue!
Red has fallen!
In its place remains a purplish blue.

Green is next,
falls to brown,
gold is the last one down.

The new colours rise,
to fight once more,
on the ever turning mirror.

Fern Riddell (12)
Barton Court Grammar School

SEASONS OF THE YEAR

Seasons come and seasons go,
Spring into summer,
Summer into autumn,
Autumn into winter.

In spring the baby lambs skip over the daffodil fields,
And birds sing from the trees,
Mother duck and her ducklings go for a long, cool swim,
While foxes play gleefully in their cool, dry den.

Summer brings happiness,
Thoughts of sandy beaches,
And children making sandcastles whilst eating refreshing ice-cream.

Autumn is a spooky month, full of witches and ghosts,
Guys burn on bonfires and sparkling fireworks are displayed,
Golden yellow or burnt-red leaves fall from the trees,
And so do conkers, horse chestnuts, acorns and helicopters.

Ho, ho, ho, Christmas at last,
Snow is falling making a white sheet upon the land,
Stockings are being filled waiting for a happy child,
And if you are a naughty child you may even see Santa in his sleigh!

Maria Pope (12)
Barton Court Grammar School

OFF THE RAILS

In the carriage of the train of life,
There's a map of the vital line,
So you'll know when you're going off the rails.
And be ready for your stop in time.
All around me children race,
But I've no answer to their shouts,
For it's better to be thought a silent fool,
Than to speak, and remove all doubt.

If the velvet seats are comfy,
If the decor's plush and nice,
If aromas waft from the lunch cart,
Smells of sugar, pastry and spice . . .
Then why do I spend the journey,
Looking out to the other side,
Staring longingly through the window
On life's endless express ride?

They say the grass is always greener,
On the other side of the fence,
But there's nothing more about that grass,
Than that I should like to walk on it hence.
And as the train enters a tunnel,
That grass is forever gone,
But life has no emergency stop cord,
And the train goes on and on.

Stephen Wicken (16)
Barton Court Grammar School

KALEIDOSCOPE

As I look through the small, black hole,
Wondering what I'll see,
Wonderful shapes and patterns,
All colours there will be.

As you turn the end of the tube,
The shapes twist around,
It's like the feeling when,
You spin around and fall onto the ground.

There are all different seasons of colours,
Summer, winter, hot and cold,
You can see the patterns clearly,
In the kaleidoscope that you hold.

Kerrie Bundock (12)
Barton Court Grammar School

IS THIS THE END?

The colours change like the seasons,
from bright and warm summers,
to cold and dark winters.
As the colours mix and match,
They blow up like fireworks.

The patterns turn without a sound,
round and round you shall go,
the patterns racing fast,
but how long will it last?
The colours are slowing down,
'Is this the end?'
I shall ask.

Angela Yue (12)
Barton Court Grammar School

KALEIDOSCOPE

I can travel to another world with my secret,
the Kaleidoscope Dragon;
I walk down his long black cave,
I see his amber tongues of flames;
He turns and I see his wings ablaze with colours,
He walks towards me, I see his dark green
scales catch the dim light;
We are standing face to face, I see his
ruby eyes glow,
He steps back and blows a cloud of silver
smoke carelessly into the humid air;
Then he disappears, and leaves me all on my own;
I turn and walk sadly back into my lonely world.

Katie Zurakovsky (12)
Barton Court Grammar School

MIRRORS

Mirrors turning,
Staring eyes.
Beautiful colours,
That are secretly disguised
When I sleep.
It's in my dreams,
Colours going round,
Haunting me.
They capture me,
Make me beg on my
Knees,
Hypnotise me
With ease.

Lucy Burt (12)
Barton Court Grammar School

MAGIC MIRRORS IN
THE KALEIDOSCOPE OF LIFE

The mirrors of the world,
Are all brought together;
Always changing,
Always moving,
In the kaleidoscope of life.

As I go through time,
I see different images;
In the mirrors,
Of the kaleidoscope of life.

My happy existence is brought back to me;
As I look into the mirrors,
Of the kaleidoscope of life.

But sometimes,
My unhappy trials of time,
Are brought back to me;
By the mirrors,
Of the kaleidoscope of life.

The kaleidoscope of life,
Is a time unrevealed;
When distant thoughts and memories,
Are brought back to mind.
Sometimes good, sometimes bad,
But the mirrors are there,
Everywhere;
Round every corner,
On every wall -
The kaleidoscope of life.

Abbie Stupple (13)
Barton Court Grammar School

CHANGING KALEIDOSCOPE

Magical moving pictures,
Changing all the time,
Colourful and bright,
Magical moving pictures,
Changing in the light.

It looks like a reflection,
Images of light,
Patterns changing as it turns,
Magical moving pictures,
Changing in the light.

Red, blue, green and yellow,
Patterns changing,
Colours moving,
Different colours emerging,
As the end moves around.

Changing magical pictures,
Moving like reflections,
Nice yet bright,
Magical moving pictures,
Changing in the light.

Aimee Humphrey (12)
Barton Court Grammar School

KALEIDOSCOPE

Kaleidoscope of colours
twisting into different shapes.
Whizzing and whirling patterns
are the effect that it makes.

Like a winding washing machine
that turns around.
A little tiny colour wheel
swirling on the ground.

Heather Ackland (12)
Barton Court Grammar School

KALEIDOSCOPE

Twisting round and round each other,
Magical mirrors in a cylinder,
Symmetrical patterns in a pretty colour,
Frustration in my heart and my soul.

It is a long black tube,
Reflection is a key,
Like a Smarties' tube,
Reminds me of a jewel.

I'm changing emotions now,
I feel happy again,
I haven't seen any brown,
I like the kaleidoscope.

It's all coming back to me,
I'm in my garden,
I'm in my tree,
No, I'm not, I'm in my room.

It's changing colours and patterns too,
It's going red,
It's going blue,
I think I'll go to bed now.
        Night!

Ryan Morrow (13)
Barton Court Grammar School

THE HUMAN MIND

Your mind's eye shows
All that you have seen
All you can imagine
All there is that's free.

The colours are flying
Around your head
The kaleidoscope is there instead.

The eagle screams
The kill is dead
And the colours still rocket
Inside your head.

Your mind is warped
The colours have gone
And all that they left
Is a memory of fun.

Matthew Rogers (12)
Barton Court Grammar School

MY KALEIDOSCOPE

Peep through the peephole
And what do you see?
Patterns down the long tunnel
Pretty as can be
Triangles and rectangles
All shapes and sizes
And what have you got?
A kaleidoscope full of surprises!

Laura Jeanes (11)
Barton Court Grammar School

THE KALEIDOSCOPE

The kaleidoscope's the thing for me,
With its shapes, colours and non-complexity.

So easy to use, they're my precious jewels,
The patterns I make when I've got the blues.

It's like a washing machine the way it goes round,
My magic mirror's never letting me down.

I feel like a wizard - the Wizard of Oz,
The way I change emotions and colours galore.

I can even change the seasons, without finding it a bore,
By turning the tube more and more.

This is my saviour when I want to escape,
And hide from the world in my dark tube of shapes.

Andy Webb (12)
Barton Court Grammar School

THE MOON

I saw one dark and starry night,
The moon, it looked all grey and white,
And though it twinkled here and there,
It looked so cold and unaware,
That millions around the globe,
Were watching it from their own homes.
I must have watched it all the night,
For soon it began to grow light,
And as it drew quite near to dawn,
I saw the dew upon the lawn.

Oliver Bolton-Fisher (11)
Barton Court Grammar School

KALEIDOSCOPE

Kaleidoscopes remind me of the night sky,
Full of shining stars.
They're like the Blackpool Illuminations,
A patchwork quilt.

A kaleidoscope is like a mini-telescope,
The lights of France when looking out from Dover.
It's like a class of shapes,
Being told where to go and what to do.

Kaleidoscopes sound like a baby's rattle,
When the shapes change position.
The patterns are symmetrical,
And they change like clothes moving around
                                    in a washing machine.

Helen Lancaster (11)
Barton Court Grammar School

KALEIDOSCOPE

K ites coloured brightly,
A lways flying high,
L oads of bright colours,
E ntering the sky.
I n my kaleidoscope, these things I see,
D o you have a kaleidoscope?
O r a kite to see?
S o why not find one,
C oloured brightly,
O h, lovely colours.
P eople I do see,
E ver looking through one like me.

Jonathan Haddock (11)
Barton Court Grammar School

KALEIDOSCOPE

Whoosh goes the windmill
As the wind blows past.
Whoosh goes the windmill
Spinning around so fast.

Colours flashing past my eyes
Orange, purple, what a delight!
Colours flashing past my eyes
Green, blue meet my sight.

Autumn leaves gathered on the ground
Swirling swiftly in the wind.
Autumn leaves gathered on the ground
A winter carpet comes to mind.

Autumn colours scattered all around
Colours of red, orange, brown and gold.
Autumn colours scattered all around
The autumn scene has been told.

Nikki Clarke (11)
Barton Court Grammar School

KALEIDOSCOPE

I put the tube to my eye
I turn the end, there is a cascade of colour
The shapes fall into place
A world through a drunken man's eyes
It turns again, there is Blackpool by night
The reds, whites and greens all blurred
I pull the tube from my eye
Away from its magical world.

Thomas Hyner (12)
Barton Court Grammar School

SAD GOODBYES

I lay calmly asleep in my bed
With the cool breeze from the fan on my head.

When suddenly 'Cock-a-doodle-doo'
As if to say 'Hey wake up you.'

So I got out of bed and shouted
'Mum we've only got an hour.'

Then I heard the water stop
And straight after the door unlock.

The sun had yet to come up
So outside was dark and still except for my pup.

Fudge was her name
Always willing for a game.

She was so close to my heart
I could not bear to think we would soon be apart.

I went outside to give her a hug
And fill her bowl with milk from a jug.

On receiving both of these
She jumped about and licked my knees.

I wandered around the house and it brought a tear to my eye
To think that this was my last goodbye.

Crystal Richardson (11)
Barton Court Grammar School

SEASONS

In the spring it is cool,
The daffodils and tulips bud,
Lambs will be born,
And will play on the soft mud.

In the summer it's the best time of year,
It is boiling hot and we can go to the beach,
It is the summer holidays,
Hooray! No school for kids
And the teachers do not have to teach.

In the autumn it gets cold,
Little children can play in the leaves,
The clock turns back by an hour,
When the wind blows, conkers fall off trees.

Finally, the winter comes,
Wrap up warm and sit in front of the log fire,
Children build snowmen out of the soft flaky snow,
Be careful not to slip on the ice, broken bones are no one's desire!

Charlotte Miles (11)
Barton Court Grammar School

KALEIDOSCOPE

Lots of colours flying around
Making a funny rattling sound
Shining, sparkling in my eye
Like stars lit up in the night sky
Fantasy, brightness, amazing me
Lots of changing colours to see
Many luminous invitations
Like Blackpool illuminations.

Tim Scott (12)
Barton Court Grammar School

KALEIDOSCOPE

K aleidoscopes, they glisten with light.
A magnificent piece of work.
L eaving you stunned in a world of magic.
E ven grown-ups are dazzled.
I ndigo, red, orange or green.
D ivine colours are these.
O ut of ten it scores the top.
S o like a patchwork quilt.
C arnival lights put into a tube.
O ur eyes must be playing tricks.
P roviding cheer for all who see it.
E ven Blackpool lights can't be compared.

Joanna Price (12)
Barton Court Grammar School

KALEIDOSCOPE

Shapes, squares, diamonds, circles,
Colours, yellow, pink and green,
They glitter and sparkle,
They light up and gleam,
Turning different colours,
Becoming different shapes,
It's weird, it's magical,
How does it work?

Natalie Brownbridge (12)
Barton Court Grammar School

KALEIDOSCOPE OF FOOD

They say I'm a fussy eater
And I suppose it's true
Staring at the huge pile of *greens*
On my plate
Makes me feel quite *blue.*

I don't like vegetable salad
Or Chilli Con Carne with rice
And you all eat your grapes and *oranges*
I'd rather eat *pink* sugar mice.

I don't like *purple* plums a lot
Though I used to when I was small
I used to eat from a paper bag
And I don't like *red* cherries at all.

I can't stand liver and onions
Or scrambled eggs or peas
And even though my sister does
I don't like *green* apples or cheese.

I don't like *white* pickled onions
I find them rather smelly
I don't like mayonnaise on chips
But I do like *yellow* jelly.

I do like chocolate *mint* ice-cream
With loads of thick *brown* chocolate sauce
And what's my favourite sandwich filling?
Strawberries and tuna of course!

Beverlie Stratton (12)
Barton Court Grammar School

KALEIDOSCOPE

Down the dark eerie tunnel,
Into a blaze of light.

A garden of flowers in spring,
Rosebuds opening to the sunlight.
All sparkling reds and glistening greens.

As spring turns to summer,
Sapphire blue fills the sky,
Soon concealed by deep emerald greens.

Summer's greens change,
To the reds and golds of autumn leaves.
Gliding to the ground.
Where flowers once stood.

The wheel at the front stops dead,
As the light shines through
Like a stained glass window.

As soon as the wheel is turned again,
Glass shatters into a thousand stars,
Shimmering, sparkling.
All scattered into space,
Slowing -
As they separate
Settling, slowly,
Slower
Still.

Rachel Kelly (11)
Barton Court Grammar School

LOOKING THROUGH A KALEIDOSCOPE

As I held the kaleidoscope up to my eye,
There is a range of bright colours each passing by.
Like a washing machine going round and round,
There is a small rattle of an ongoing sound.

The patterns are amazing and never alike,
It's much more exciting than getting a bike.
There are plenty of different shapes galore,
Triangles, rectangles, squares and much more.

Tara Macey (11)
Barton Court Grammar School

THE WORLD OF THE KALEIDOSCOPE

Round and round like a washing machine
Colours of precious jewels turning around
Patterns once there, then gone forever
The planets and stars dancing in time
Symmetry formed by mirrors drifting into the distance
Flowers, stars, once there but never seen again.

Emily Ward (13)
Barton Court Grammar School

Colours

In my kaleidoscope I can see
Ever changing patterns, each reminding me
Of colourful pictures in my mind,
Seen for a second then left behind.

Blue for a boy, pink for a girl,
Caramel's a delicious chocolate swirl.
Green is the springtime from the brown earth,
Reminding us of nature's continuous rebirth.

Black for sorrow, we shed a tear,
Red for danger and for fear.
Crimson blood at the scene of a crime,
Grey in the beard of Old Father Time.

Autumn brings a golden hue,
Yellow, orange and scarlet to name but a few
Of the wonderful colours, before winter's dark days,
But white is the snow where Santa sleighs.

Silver's the tinsel to hang on the tree,
Gold are the baubles that twinkle with glee.
Claret's the wine that's poured in the glass,
All seen for a second as they fade and pass.

Charlotte Pateman (12)
Barton Court Grammar School

CHRISTMAS DAY

All cosy, dozing in my bed,
Suddenly Zoë jumps on my head,
Excited as an elf on this day,
Desperate for Christmas to be underway.
We creep down lighted stairs to see what's there,
The smell of roasting turkey fills the air,
And everywhere is
Joy and happiness.
Laughter and fun after Christmas dinner,
Relatives going home for another year,
Satisfied from wine and beer.
Children heading for their beds,
Adults resting their weary heads,
Another Christmas Day is done.

Katy Jackson (12)
Beechwood Sacred Heart School

WARTIME CRIES!

Yet another bombshell drops,
The whole street, the whole world stops.
If you listen carefully, there are cries.
Another house, another family dies.
Today is today and not any other.
Another lonely child, without a father or a mother.
He plays on his own, he has no friends, they are dead.
His clothes are torn, he bleeds from a cut on the head.
He finds himself a place to rest, he wakes in pain.
He must have been captured during the night.
He is bleeding, he's in jail, it starts to rain.
How could they? How dare they? What right?

Theresa Danagher-Smith (14)
Beechwood Sacred Heart School

MY BEST FRIEND

I walked to the breakfast table,
The 'Daily Times' in my hand.
Then the headlines hit me,
'Girl disappeared in the sand.'

Her name was once Anne Jones.
She had been my very best friend.
So close, we were inseparable,
Right up till the very end.

We met when I moved from Australia,
She showed me round the first grade.
The others made fun of my accent,
But as my friend she stayed.

I sat at the breakfast table,
The 'Daily Times' in my hand.
The headlines stared up at me,
My best friend had died in the sand.

Abby Kennedy (12)
Beechwood Sacred Heart School

WINTER

I saw upon a winter's day,
A squirrel run through the wood.
Watching. Waiting.
It stopped and stood
Hiding behind a bush.
The squirrel had no fear,
And it ran off when the coast was clear.

Amy Greenwood (14)
Beechwood Sacred Heart School

I Love Cats

Cats, cats I love,
Cats, cats with paws like gloves.
Claw the furniture, scratch the bed,
Sleepy cats yawn instead.

Cats, cats stare at fish,
Cats, cats eat from a dish,
Climb the trees, and run through grass,
Catching flies as they pass.

Cats, cats curled up tight,
Cats, cats purring at night.
Licking themselves all around,
I love listening to their sound.

Alia Hassan (12)
Beechwood Sacred Heart School

The Sweet Shop

As I enter the sweet shop,
I aim for a lollipop.
The shop decorated in soft pink,
I realise sweets and I have a link.
Imagine what the dentist would say,
If he saw how many sweets I eat a day.
My favourite would have to be chewy toffee,
I do admit to disliking the fudge coffee.
Another favourite would have to be liquorice allsorts,
As sweets are always in my thoughts.
I really should take note of my Uncle Keith,
As due to sweets his mouth is full of false teeth.

Carla MacGregor (12)
Beechwood Sacred Heart School

LIFE

I know I'm falling into a spiral of shame,
whispers and pain are always on my brain.
I'm sitting here alone in a corner
feeling the emptiness of life as a loner.
My eyes never open, my heart never alight,
wishing one day it would go out of sight.
I know now what it feels like
knowing it will always give me a fright.
My emotions are dying,
my life uninspiring.
One day I wish it would come to an end.
It aches and it hurts
and it makes me feel like dirt.
One day I know it will tear me apart.
It is black.
As black as my heart.

Celia Beale (13)
Beechwood Sacred Heart School

THE FUTURE

Different in every imagination,
Silver dust swirling around us.
What is virtual and what is real?
No one knows and no one cares.
Robots dominate, terrorise.
Computers rule the world.
A time bomb ticks under the ocean
Ready to explode at any moment.
Future . . .? What future?

Emily Mason (12)
Beechwood Sacred Heart School

MY TV

My TV is the best thing
that ever happened to me.
I can go anywhere without
leaving my chair.
I can go on safari or
drive the latest Ferrari.
There is a whole world in
there and I do not have
to leave my chair.

I can fly to the moon,
see my sweetheart and swoon.
Deep sea diving,
Formula One driving,
do anything I dare
without leaving my chair.

Tessa Fry (12)
Beechwood Sacred Heart School

CANDY STICK

Long and twirly,
Red and white.
Twisting, curling,
A delicious bite.

Candy sticks,
I love them all,
More and more,
Just make me drool.

Stephanie Barnett (11)
Beechwood Sacred Heart School

COLOURS

We take colours for granted,
Look at the sky knowing
That it will always be blue.
Always ready to cheer you up.
But what if you got up one day,
Opened the curtains and
The sky was black.
Everything was black and
There were no red poppies
Or a bright sun in the sky.
What would we do?

Alexine Bullett (13)
Beechwood Sacred Heart School

A HUG

It's wondrous what a hug can do,
A hug can say, *I like you.*
A hug can say, *I love you so,*
Or, *gee I hate to see you go.*
A hug can say, *cheer up friend,*
You know the world isn't at an end.
A hug can say, *welcome back,*
Or, *I wish you good luck.*
So open your arms without delay,
And give someone a hug today.

Natasha Shamutete (13)
Beechwood Sacred Heart School

COLOURS OF THE WORLD

Colours bring us sadness and joy
They define the difference between girl and boy.
Happiness is bright and light,
Sadness is dark and lonely.
Orange, yellow, red and brown
All you have to do is look around.
They're everywhere, we just do not care!
Summer colours, autumn colours, winter and spring.
They give us life, that's what they bring.

Jenny Gray (13)
Beechwood Sacred Heart School

A DREAM TO BE SHATTERED

The purity of life,
The hope for eternal love.
Battles my soul keeps fighting,
Wars my mind will never conquer.
I want unity with everyone;
Compassion felt together.
A connection of life's soul,
Each heart beating as one.
We are one being.
We hate and taunt each other,
So therefore we hate ourselves.
We mock one another
And criticise who we are.
Everyone is undercover,
Who are we disguising ourselves for?
Let society break free,
Before the life we know becomes a cage.

Stephanie Whitelaw (15)
Cranbrook School

Old Woman

'I haven't seen you for a long time.'
She quivered.
A thin rivulet of dribble
Running from her cleft lip.
Furtive tissue dabbing indiscriminately.
'I don't get out much now.
Used to see you when I walked my dog,
Then my husband died.'
She has large warts
Aligned on her neck.
Warts peculiar to old age.
'Do you still have the dog?' I enquire.
'Oh, that got run over.'
Eyes momentarily misting with
Unwept tears.
Unwept because tears
No longer concern her.
'I don't get out much now'
I nod in feigned sympathy I am
Unable to feel.
The cup is raised shakily,
Quivering lips expecting, yet not anticipating
It's warmth.
The hand starts back.
Polka dot coffee stains on the tablecloth,
Mostly dried.
She's sitting alone now, as always.
An elderly yet auburn-haired woman
Comes to help her up,
Hand trawling for the bag next to her feet.
Stands bowed over the chair,
Zimmer frame springing to well oiled life.

Her thick ankles stumble over mown grass,
Wrists shaking under her weight.
A cripple.
'I don't get out much now.'

Lettie Ransley (13)
Cranbrook School

THE YEAR

In springtime the weather is fine
And the birds come back to flock in their nests.
The French are preparing the grapes for wine
But we all know that Australian's best.

In the summer, everyone is going away
Greece, Italy, America and Spain,
But not me I'd rather stay
Than fly at 30,000 feet on a plane.

In the autumn, when the weather is getting bad
And people are starting to feel the cold,
The prices in the shops make people mad
And they don't give to appeals for the old.

In the wintertime, when presents are bought
And Christmas is finally here.
The families rejoice and know that they ought
To wish in this Happy New Year!

Richard Batchelor (16)
Cranbrook School

FACING DEATH - THE LOVER, THE ENEMY

For the first time I feel the light dimming, like a
Far away star growing weaker and distant.
The truths that drew us together are upon you now
And the cruel irony of it tears us apart, so threatening
And unreal. The pain I see to understand in your eyes
Wounds me as I try to lift your weight from you.
The loneliness seems inevitable as I look into your
Heart finding there the memory and experience that
Belong to me, that belong to us.

As you believe to feel the end of this spiralling
Staircase I stand with you, by your victorious mind,
But defeated body. Through your burden you have
Come to trust no other as I have come to love no
Other. I see your face and hear your sweet voice as I
Close my eyes. Knowing that one day I will be with
You again, comforts me.

For the first time I feel I have come to know you
Too well. As I have delved into your mind and soul,
You have devoured me. I became you. The harm I
Caused was intentionally to protect you, but it failed
And now you lie in the arms of death reaching for the
Light which has become so distant; for me also. I too
Have faced extinction from the depths of recognition
Falling into a darkness.

My faith is shaken as I see you look upon your loved
Ones. I long to stand around you also, to feel the
Warmth of your eyes, but all I see is a glaze of fire.
My memories are twisted as I wind backwards into a
Depth of guilt which began with you. I turn to face you.
Forgive me.

Sarah Sterling (16)
Cranbrook School

ANGER

Anger is like a raging tornado,
Spinning around in your head.
It's like a storm pounding your mind.

Anger is like a raging river,
Crashing round the rocks.
It's like pebbles battering your brain.

Anger is like a raging bull,
Snorting in the ring.
It's like your head is in a china shop.

Anger is like a raging fire,
Burning in your brain.
It's like a kettle coming to the boil.

Anger is like a steam train,
Charging down the track.
It's like steam coming out of your ears.

Terry Butcher (11)
Dover Grammar School For Boys

YO-YO

The yo-yo, runs as swiftly as a stream,
Spins like a whirlwind,
Swings like a pendulum,
Up and down like a roller-coaster.

Lights up as if it was a lamppost,
The string as smooth as silk,
Sounds like a bomb or a bee,
A whirling tornado, a swirling hurricane.

Simon Lawfull (11)
Dover Grammar School For Boys

HAPPINESS

Winning the lottery,
Ruling a country,
Playing football for England,
Or just having fun.
Eating all the chocolate I can,
On a tropical island.
Swimming in a pool of banana
milkshake,
When you're feeling happy there's
nothing better.

Ben Punton (11)
Dover Grammar School For Boys

FEAR

At night I am falling,
Falling into darkness.
The wind rushes past my face.
As I descend the darkness surrounds me,
It seizes me, and twists me.
Then it lets go.
I am now rising,
I look up and see a light.
And then I awake,
Panting and gasping for air.

Gareth Hewer (11)
Dover Grammar School For Boys

GRANDAD'S WATCH

It is midnight,
I look at my watch,
It is my grandad's watch,
He gave it to me
As a present to remember him.
It reminds me of him
And I miss him so much.
The war brought me to England
But left him in Yugoslavia.
On the back of the watch I feel
The letters deeply engraved.
('Adusu od deda'?)
'To Adis from his grandad'.

Adis Dobardzic (11)
Dover Grammar School For Boys

HAPPINESS

Winning the lottery
Rolling in gold
Bathing in chocolate
Driving a Rolls.

Fishing for jewellery
Eating marshmallows
Owning a mansion
Flying through meadows.

Nathan Allen (11)
Dover Grammar School For Boys

CAP BADGE - YORK AND LANCASTER

York and Lancaster
it says on the banner,
beneath the tiger bright.
The tiger ready to pounce
hunches his back
searching for prey
in his domain.
From the banner bursts
laurel leaves,
reaching for the crown.
The Tudor Rose,
crowned in all its might,
is vanishing from sight.
The crown above,
soiled with age.
The clip is no more,
broken through time.

In the past,
the clip was there,
clipped on a cap with pride.
The soldier to whom it belonged,
on a battlefield died.
Though he was never known to me,
I treasure his memory,
through the cap badge.

David Harper (11)
Dover Grammar School For Boys

TERROR

Black is the colour of terror
In a haunted spooky house,
Terrifying, dangerous and very mysterious
Dark, silent and scary.

Red is the colour of terror
The colour of scarlet blood,
Rushing from a bloody nose
Falling like a waterfall.

White is the colour of terror
The colour of a spooky ghost,
Haunting you for eternal life
A dark trailing shadow.

Mark Jenkins (11)
Dover Grammar School For Boys

THE MEMENTO

Bought long ago by a soldier for a few rupees,
Lovingly hammered and carved to shape,
Sold by a native Indian peasant,
Sailed through storms and across oceans,
A memento of a great war.
Ganesha the God of good luck,
Glitters in the bright sunlight,
His fat belly symbolising the prosperity he brings.
He sits silent guarding everyone, as he always will.

Kenneth Birmingham (11)
Dover Grammar School For Boys

LOVE MELODIES, ON A WINTER'S DAY

(A parody of Christopher Marlowe's 'Passionate Shepherd')

Come glide with me upon the ice,
With gifts so rare, I shall entice.
Frozen lakes, sugar crystals,
Silk sheets flutter on the steeples.

And we shall dream on mounds of snow,
Seeing the glistening dewdrops glow.
Where mountain peaks lay undisturbed,
A satin secret we shall observe.

And I will show you glacier sparkles,
Share secrets encased in marble.
An icicle pendant holds our love,
A sudsy white sky hovers above.

A crown of glass, embedded jewels,
As silver as the gold for fools.
Dancing slippers shimmer sweet,
Embroidered toes for fragile feet.

A river bank of lily white,
The Snow Queen's kiss, a bitter bite.
If these delights make you think twice,
Still glide with me upon the ice.

Beyond our vision, through a haze,
The winter picture, tearful glaze.
If these delights make you think thrice,
Then glide with me upon the ice.

Aimée V Baker (13)
Fort Pitt Grammar School For Girls

WATER WOMAN'S EXPRESSIVE LOVE
(A parody of Christopher Marlowe's 'Passionate Shepherd')

Come glide with me under water rays,
And leave your troubles behind always.
Closely we'll lie under sandy covers,
We'll be together, eternal lovers.

Exotic colours from a rainbow are thrust.
These shine through the water rays sparkling with dust.
Shining, shimmering, come see the sights,
Harbour lanterns on moonlit nights.

Pearls confined in silky shells,
Will show your future wedding bells.
To you I give the sweetest pearl,
Wrapped in silk from the greatest Earl.

Scaly gowns from tropical fish,
Presented on a silver dish.
Tiaras made with the steadiest hand,
These can be seen from a distant land.

Treasures golden all glistening below,
Padlocked cases displayed on show.
Surprises, delights all so secure,
Like our love together, wholesome and pure.

Come glide with me under water rays,
We'll never go our separate ways.
Oh lift me high in your powerful arms,
And I shall change to meet your charms.

Phillippa Phipps (13)
Fort Pitt Grammar School For Girls

THE ARDENT MERMAN TO HIS LOVER

(A parody of Christopher Marlowe's 'Passionate Shepherd')

Come swim with me and take my hand,
I'll take you to a distant land,
Where castles rise up through the air,
And pretty maidens comb their hair.

And we shall dance upon the tide,
Watching boats crash as they glide,
Through unseen boulders in their throng,
Then we shall sing our mournful song.

Alas to you I will bestow,
An opal pendant from below
The caves of shining fantasy
Engraved with love for all to see.

A woven robe of purest silk,
Which from our pretty worms we milk,
Richly lined with creamy pearls,
That glisten through your tumbling curls

A crown of rainbow coral stones,
Encrusted thick with golden tones.
Dear queen of all my heart and mind,
Come swim with me and take my hand.

Fish of sea and ocean floor,
Shall dance for you forever more,
If you love this kingdom grand
Then swim with me and take my hand.

Lucy Jackson (14)
Fort Pitt Grammar School For Girls

FAIRGROUND

(A parody of Christopher Marlowe's 'Passionate Shepherd')

Come laugh with me, and be my joy,
We shall play like little boys.
On the dodgems at the fair,
The glitzy lights fly everywhere.

The carousel the coconut shy.
The fortune teller who tells no lies.
We shall gaze with delight,
At the wonders of this night.

I give to you a glittering goldfish,
Darting around its pool of life.
A colourful box, a tasty treat,
A box of popcorn salted or sweet.

And I will shoot those targets down,
So you will have the finest gown,
Made of cotton and the prettiest silk,
To compliment your skin of milk.

Candyfloss gloves for the cold,
Warm and sticky in your hold.
For these pleasures be not coy,
Come laugh with me and be my joy.

The fairground people show the way,
In which to have a lovely day.
If this presents a pleasing ploy,
Come laugh with me and share my joy.

Ann Elizabeth Ratcliffe (13)
Fort Pitt Grammar School For Girls

FORESTS

For all the things that you can see,
Forests are the things for me.

Over plains and heathlands far,
Little foals are born.

Rabbits, rabbits rushing round,
Everywhere there is no sound.

Sun glistens through the trees,
Trees of all varieties.

Some grow big, some grow small,
Some don't get very far at all.

Jade E Edwards (11)
Fort Pitt Grammar School For Girls

COLOURED HOUSE

Red bricks on the drive
Brown front door
Blue, red and green in the stained glass
Blue, grey, green - carpet on the stairs
Follow the white wallpaper to the blue and white door
My bedroom
Dark blue carpet
Blue walls white ceiling
Green snooker table
But there on the walls
Posters
Red
Red Devils
Manchester United.

Peter Humphrey (17)
Grange Park College

TEENAGE CRISIS

Being a teenager's a very hard job:
This is when old people start calling you 'Yob'!
When your favourite saying is, 'It's just not fair.'
Or, 'That's bang out of order,' or, 'I just don't care.'
When your parents hearing sensitivity seems to increase,
Though maximum volume is your idea of peace.
When your brother or sister become obnoxious creeps,
But, though you don't like it, you've got them for keeps.
When you're big enough to wear your dad's clothes, but won't.
When you're old enough to do the ironing, but don't.
When your dad's head looks like a bit of bum fluff,
Just remember, you'll be like him soon enough.

Stuart Burke (14)
Hugh Christie Technology College

SUICIDE BY DROWNING

I jump,
Then fall deep beneath the crashing waves
The world above me drifting away.
Happiness flows between my fingers and toes,
Freedom lingers at the ocean floor.
I struggle and try to scream as the life inside me starts to die,
Bubbles of air drift away from me, taking my memories with them.
The adventurous water squeezes the air from me,
My body fills with the water's emotions,
There I lie on the ocean floor,
With no worries for me,
No more . . .

Sara Werren (14)
Hugh Christie Technology College

THE DARK MAN

He is the Devil's advocate,
Cunning and slender,
His hair sways in the night air as he watches from the rooftops.
He is the ultimate sportsman,
He picks the ones that are strong and healthy,
Others like him use only the weak and helpless.
He is a chronic insomniac,
Even when he sleeps he is watching all,
Rising only at night to scour the city.
He is the shadows,
His blood-red pupils scanning the night's new faces,
He sees a worthy catch,
Her pale face shining from the others,
Pale,
Innocent,
Alone.
He is judge and jury:
Descending on the victim,
She knows not why or how her life is to end,
But he knows her fate.
He is the Grim Reaper,
Dealing the death card,
His victim lifeless and cold with staring eyes,
Her tomb is to be a back street gutter.
He is executioner.
He is an artist,
In his trail he leaves a host of carefully hidden bodies,
As he paints the city,
Ready for the crimson dawn,
When he sleeps once more,
And the mourners awake to face their losses.

James Stringer (14)
Hugh Christie Technology College

A VOLCANO

Natural disasters
Grand or petite.
Sleepy mountains, peaceful islands.
Capable of appearing on land or sea,
Wherever they are situated mayhem will be.
Time slowly progresses,
A year, a lifetime or even a hundred,
It will explode,
But when?
Only time will tell.

When the volcano begins to spit,
Rumbling, waking from a slumber.
The ground shudders in protest,
Lava spews from its vent.
A warning to its neighbours,
To be taken or ignored.
It won't wait for your decision.

After the blast life becomes a thing of the past.
An angry overflow of change hungry and unstoppable seeps
down eating all it sees.
The fiery river cuts the land into a new shape leaving cold
hard ash as a reminder.
Those that stood proud, defying the volcano, daring to remain
are consumed.
The belching gases and smoke linger like a veil of destruction
as the volcano falls quiet.
It sleeps but its brief activity leaves an eternal mark.
Until the next time . . .

Simon Bridgeman (13)
Hugh Christie Technology College

THE ROAD THROUGH

Out through the darkness, embraced by the light.
The shape of innocence will go from sight.
The further you go, the harder it seems.
You look around, you see the fields and streams.
You can't stop now, you have so far to go.
Things are changing, it is starting to show.
At times you feel tired, you need to refill.
Image of mist echoes the window sill.
It hits you, doors open and they can shut.
It can bless you then kick you in the gut.
A natural progression can cause a shock.
Along the way you may meet a road block.
You ease into a state, no one's around.
The gates of underworld, you meet breakdown.

Mark Seabourne (14)
Hugh Christie Technology College

PREMONITION TO A WEDDING

Before the time I go hand in hand to be wed,
Over my flowers this chant I shall shed.
The one whom this bouquet shalt catch,
Start her out to meet her match.
But if she should have ill at heart,
Her lover and she should be set apart.

Do not in this, make a blunder,
True lovers should never be torn asunder.
For those who have ill in mind,
In matters of love should be set behind.

Kate Morgan (15)
Hugh Christie Technology College

THE MASK

I'm painting a picture.
An empty slate for me to fill,
a brand new page for me to explore!
A face!
The curves, the eyes, the nose, and lips,
waiting for their new result.
The pinks, the browns, the cream and sponge.
The finished product with a smile.
The foundation begins to layer on,
dabbing with a sponge,
blusher brushed across the cheeks,
creates a new sensation.
Eyes begin to take their shape,
lashes long and curly.
Lips look lush and ready to kill,
my painting's almost done.
My empty slate is now full of wonder,
ready to be shown.
Now with confidence, out the room,
my painting gets admired.

Emma Lake (15)
Hugh Christie Technology College

FLYING

High up in the sky,
like a hot air balloon.
Flying up so high,
reaching the top soon.

Seeing the trees below,
and the hovering clouds rise.
Up in the sky is where I'd like to go,
making the land below look out of size.

Speedily high above,
flit, flutter, hover, soar.
Flying like a dove,
I'm flying out the door.

Darting rapidly high,
I'm flying in the sky.

Emma Fiorentini (13)
Hugh Christie Technology College

FIRE

Fiery heat of the hot
living monstrous flames that
steal the powers from around them

Mystical colours of the
magical powers that live
inside of the burning fire

Monstrous living colours of
the mystical magic that is heat
fire and life in one.

Chris Davis (13)
Hugh Christie Technology College

THE THING I LOVE TO DO

The speed builds up as you rush down a steep hill.
The bumps that try to throw you off.
The ruts they draw you into your doom.
The sharp bends that appear to go straight.
The gravel sliding around under your wheels.
The trees that you weave in and out of.
The wet leaves pull your wheels away.
The steps that drop further and further away.

Then it all goes wrong and you hit something.
You soar through the air, falling, falling then bang.
You hit the dirt and slide to a dramatic stop.
The wet muddy puddle seeps into your clothes.
You feel annoyed as you get up.
The water runs off your clothes and forms another puddle.
Luckily you aren't hurt so you get back on and carry on riding.
Cycling, I love it.

Daniel Walker (14)
Hugh Christie Technology College

DREAM BIKE

The appearance of it and the scent of the leather pulls you towards it,
The chrome shimmering in the blazing sun,
The leather scorches you as you touch it,
Then as you rotate the key,
It bursts into life with a lovely roar,
It's a Harley Davidson.

Jonathan Saxby (14)
Hugh Christie Technology College

FRENCH TROOPS RESTING

15 brave men
Sitting worried, scared
15 brave men
Thinking wild thoughts
15 brave men
Will they return home?
15 brave men
When will they next fight?
Fighting so glorified by the press
And the outside world but these
15 brave men know it's not
15 brave men
Shaking with fright, stormed with nightmares and
Frightening thoughts, what will the next corner bring?
Death or salvation
15 brave men
Trapped in death, destruction and pain
15 brave men trapped.

Alex Vanstone (13)
Hugh Christie Technology College

RED SOLDIERS

Red shining armour which is gleaming in the sun,
soldiers lining up for a duty to be done.
The mass on their horseback queuing in a line,
flags flying high as they stand their ground.
The enemy in sight,
their hearts start to pound,
the shout goes out,
as they start to advance,
a spear,
a shield,
a shot rings out,
many think of home as their body hits the ground.
Shadows are appearing,
soldiers are leaving,
swords are flying high as the silver reflects the sky.
Horses standing, shadowed by the orange dusk.
Men retreating home,
a casual glance behind,
their war is done,
with loss of limb they wonder how it all begun.

Mark Dyer (13)
Hugh Christie Technology College

The Subway

It's like another world down there,
As I walk down the gloomy stair.
The walls are atrocious,
Full of dirt and grime,
Smells, graffiti, heat and noise.

Broadway - Harlem - Wall Street - 5th Avenue.

There in the corner stands a gruesome man,
With a funny yellowy-orange tan.
He's got holes in his trousers,
Disgraceful spots on his head,
Shocking, foul, horrid.

Brooklyn - Rockefeller Center - Queens.

It's like another world down there,
Enter it if you dare.
The noise is ear-piercing,
As the train slams down its breaks.
At last I'm here, at my place.

Emily Stone (13)
Hugh Christie Technology College

SCREAM

Feel it coming
Forcing its way up and up
Wondering whether it'll be a
Bawl
Holler
Screech
Yelp
Shriek
Shrill
Or squeal

                    Will it be an
                    Earth shattering
                    Earthquake starter
                    Glass shattering
                    Window breaking
                    Eardrum bursting
                    Outcry?

Now the sensation is over
Ears still ringing
Earth still trembling . . .

Silence.

Jaime Harris (13)
Hugh Christie Technology College

DUNBLANE

This happened at Dunblane Primary School, upon a normal day,
The children came into the grounds and started there to play.

When the little school bell rang, the children all went in,
For one class in particular, the first lesson was gym.

When those children had got changed and gone into the gym,
They started to run and jump, just doing the normal thing.

Those children were just having fun, doing what children do best,
Innocent children just playing around, in their pants and vests.

Whilst nobody was watching, a man came passing by,
Looking through all the nooks and crannies, like a private spy.

He crept into the building, sneaked in the front gate,
They never saw him coming, until it was too late.

He pulled out the deadly murderous weapon, wanting to cause strife,
They never saw him coming, he meant to end their life.

He spun round with the venomous weapon, shooting all the time,
The children ducked and tried to run, it was such a terrible crime.

The madman then turned the gun on himself and pulled the trigger tight,
He fell on the floor, alive no more, what a terrible sight.

The ambulance came, the police as well, they couldn't believe what
they saw,
They picked up the dead and the injured, and hoped that there weren't
any more.

Parents rushed to the little school, not believing their eyes,
They all hoped that their children weren't dead, for some there was a
surprise.

In the end seventeen people died, sixteen children and their teacher,
The press all took advantages, and Dunblane was a daily feature.

This is now all in the past, and peace has returned to Dunblane,
It was such a tragedy waiting to happen, let's hope it doesn't happen
again.

Amy-Eleanor Stamp (13)
Highworth Grammar School

THE SCHOOL SCRAP

I'm scared to go to school today,
I could get him back I thought; no way!
As I walked into the biggish playground,
Everybody stopped but made no sound.
The boy turned round and looked at me,
He had a cut upon his knee.
It started out in the school gym,
When I'd leaned out, and I'd punched him.
Then he turned round and did the same,
Everybody watching thought it was a great game.
Then I'd lashed out, kicked him hard,
He stumbled back into the yard.
A teacher came in, Mr Core,
'Don't!' he shouted, *'Stop, no more!'*
Then the boy, I'd ripped his coat,
Got off the floor and went for my throat!
The fight went on for a few minutes or so,
At the end I had a sore leg, arm and toe!
It could have been a difficult day,
But we shook hands and went away!

Emma Grove (13)
Invicta Grammar School

THE COOLEST OF THE COOL

As water I flowed
In a long blue line
I was graceful and gentle
Clean and kind
I moved along rivers
And down long streams
Before I was water
Before I was free

But then I was trapped
And put in cube shapes
Escape was impossible
I was too late
Sacrificed to the freezer
For the rest of my life
To grow cold and chilled
And soon become ice

And now as I sit
With a bottle of milk
We freeze together
And hope they feel guilt
I froze before her
In little cube shapes
I'm cold and I'm trapped
In this confined space

Now I'm a prisoner
Now I'm not free
Chilled is my life
The cold controls me
Cramped up in a space
With no space of my own
They've taken the milk
And I am alone!

Polly Fetherstonhaugh (13)
Invicta Grammar School

THE STRANGER

He strolled through the park passing on by,
Slowly dragging his feet across the square,
Keeping his eyes fixed on the ground,
As he finds a place to sleep.

He couldn't weep, he is too brave, but why?
Doesn't he have a friend?
The wind whistled through the trees,
The leaves began to fall.

A squirrel leaped from behind a hedge,
The stranger began to turn,
'A chestnut for my squirrel friend' whispered the stranger.

Why . . . He does have a friend!

Caroline Coates (13)
Invicta Grammar School

WINTER

Winter is bursting full of fun and games
Joyous children, laughs, sweet chuckles
Thinking of their homely fireplace flames
Warming their frozen feet, hands and knuckles
Snowballs rolled in perfect spherical shape
Are thrown at youngsters running fast and free
On the landscape where the snow gently drapes
As it gradually falls on the trees
Everyone sings, dances delightfully
As people skate upon the frozen lake
Every snowman is made imperfectly
By hands of children proud of what they make
The carpeted winter ground swiftly melts
As softly, the distant sunbeams are felt.

Sarah Stevenson (14)
Invicta Grammar School

SATAN'S LOCK UP

The long chains clank around my feet,
Reminding me of the brutality I had caused,
Then there's quiet and the hollow room closes,
Closes in around me,
The footsteps of the guard and his keys,
Echoes down the hall,
And then . . .
My heart is beating faster,
I'm screaming out the words,
Trapped,
I'm trapped.

Lisa Iannidinardo (13)
Invicta Grammar School

THE WORLD, US AND SPARE

Are there other worlds, or is there just one?
The universe is in complete silence
The stars are bright, the brightest is the sun
The sheer space is free of all violence
There is no light, but sun and there's no wind
And nothing is to be heard but emptiness
Moon can make an eclipse, the world is dimmed
Earth for humans, is just a living nest
Scurrying round in their own little ways
Nobody knows what happens in space
Down on Earth the small children play
The moon really does seem to have a face
If the sun was not there, there would be no light
If the Earth was not there, there would be no life.

Karen Judge (14)
Invicta Grammar School

DEATH

Sitting alone in a black nothing,
Hardly able to breathe.
The pain torments me,
I'm trapped in a cage.
Save me from this torture,
Take me to a good place.
Take me away from this hell,
Haven't I suffered enough?

When will death come?

Cassie Dodd (13)
Invicta Grammar School

SPECIAL FEELING

Love is when you get that special feeling
You see that someone in a unique way.
It's something that your life has been missing
Those special words we both wanted to say.
Anything, just to be together
You walked away from where we both stood
You'd always said our love was forever
I thought we had something really good.
The wonderful times that we both had
The little secrets that we both shared
I cannot say it was all that bad
I really did think that you actually cared
It'll take a while to get over you
But all my feelings for you were true.

Amy Baker (14)
Invicta Grammar School

THE EVENING

The dusky blue of evening
The crystal light of the stars
The waves lapping on the beach
My safe haven they do reach.

Alone in a stony cave
The dank air that fills my nose
I lay huddled upon the ground
The shining drops of water all around.

Becky Cressy (13)
Invicta Grammar School

ANGELS

Do angels exist floating in heaven
On fluffy clouds with a silver lining?
Or couldn't possibly be cloud seven?
Up here in the sky no one is whining
Spirits of people go floating above
Not one angel fights, we all get along
Sweet dreams of floating like wings of a dove
Everybody can sing sweet angel song
Do we all have a guardian angel?
Or is that untrue, not many can tell
Looking down on us, keeping us stable
Is there a heaven or is there a hell?
I think that angels are great fragile things
Which float around with glistening wings.

Jo Bedford (14)
Invicta Grammar School

MUMS

Mums are things you cannot buy,
Like fluffy clouds in the sky,
Every mum has jobs to do,
Like sweep the house and clean the loo.

Although mums are very good housekeepers,
They sometimes need to close their peepers,
To take a rest for a minute or two,
And take a break from cleaning the loo.

I love my mum right up to Mars,
And she says she loves me to the moon and stars.

Sacha Burek (13)
Invicta Grammar School

The Last Hunt

There it was, a blur in the sunset,
It seemed as though it was waiting for something.

Its back was almost flat on the ground,
And its tail was banging from side to side.

Suddenly a herd of gazelles came rushing past,
The animal leapt up and reached 60 miles an hour in 3 seconds flat.

The cheetah picked out one gazelle,
It seemed to be the weaker one.

After a long and tiring chase,
The gazelle collapsed to the floor.

The herd of gazelles raced off,
Not caring for the poor animal.

The cheetah was just about to sink his teeth into the gazelle,
When the gunshot was heard.

All was silent and a man came from the bushes,
The gazelle ran in fear and the cheetah never hunted again.

Helen Robertson (11)
Invicta Grammar School

The Jungle

Jumpy monkeys, swinging excitedly through the leafy trees.
Unknown to his victim, the lion stalks his prey.
Nature at its best, separate from the world.
Gorillas together in harmony, hear their mating call.
Lionesses group together, nurturing their cubs.
Everything is quiet, the hunter has found his gun.

Sarah Dearling (13)
Invicta Grammar School

TRUE LOVE?

How do you know if this is true love?
Am I supposed to read a sign from you?
A pointless message from a snow-white dove
That explains everything I'm supposed to do.
Everyone said we were made for each other
But a space in my mind had uncertainty.
You said we'd be together forever,
And that we would last for eternity.
All those nights I spent on the phone to you.
So many feelings I kept deep inside.
I've never experienced love so true,
Too many feelings, I just could not hide.
I know what I've always wanted to say,
Only now do I know that you're here to stay.

Jayne Pearce (14)
Invicta Grammar School

THE OCEAN

O   ars float on the tranquil blue water,
C   rashing waves hit the dark gloomy rocks,
E   verlasting it carries on and on towards the horizon,
A   nother day it looks the same, flowing peacefully along its way,
                                    capturing everything in its reach,
N   ever ending it rushes past in a hurry towards its
                            unknown destination.

Katie Coleman (14)
Invicta Grammar School

INFESTATION

(A poem to warn unobservant mums)

Once upon a time there was
A mother, who was great, because
She never told her children to:
'Wash your face!' as others do
Or 'Clean your room!' or 'Make your bed!'
These sentences were *never* said.

By and by her kids got smelly,
As they just sat and watched the telly.
Until one day her fate befell her
And no one really dared to tell her . . .

Her kids had *fleas* and what is worse
Their rooms were infested with the curse.
She found out soon and she said 'Damn!
I'll have to call the Rentokil man!'

And so with a cleaner house she made
Her children wash - the smell would fade.
The kids, they really didn't care
And sort of 'forgot' to wash their hair.
They ended up with nits and then
The process started all over again!

Alyson Mahoney (13)
Invicta Grammar School

THE POEM THAT'S NOT A POEM

I really want to write a poem
But I can't think what to say
So I've just written anything down
And sent it in anyway.

Sarah Hicks (13)
Invicta Grammar School

THE AIR RAID

The dreaded sound of a raid as we run into the cold, damp shelter.
Spectacular flashes of light.
Wardens shouting,
People screaming at the thought of what is to come.
The sky is raining bombs and there's blackness all around.
I stand frozen still, not knowing what has happened.
I listen to the aeroplanes roar,
And the banging of the bombs.
The glass shatters and debris flies.
Then suddenly as quickly as they came,
The bombers were gone.
I closed my eyes and stepped outside.
When I opened them, all I could see was a pile of
Bricks and rubble where my house used to lie!
It feels like the only light in the world is
Coming from the fire that burns down the road.
I sit and weep as the all-clear goes.
My mother and father come out and stare,
And suddenly the blazing fire,
Creeps down to the house next door.
Put it out! Put it out!
The people roar,
At last the havoc is dying down
And the air raid is over.

Karen Barber (12)
Invicta Grammar School

ALONE

The cold feeling creeps up my spine,
Once again I sit alone,
Hearing the laughter of children outside,
Remembering.
The fire glows, but brings no happiness.
Sitting in the same old chair,
Sleeping in the same old bed,
The dusty, dark room,
Feeling depressed, hurting inside.
People walk by,
But no wave, no smile,
Trying to figure out why it happens to me,
No one cares, they're young and free,
Unlike me,
Alone.
My bones creak as I reach for the album,
The sepia prints,
Smiles then.
My family, my loved ones.
Tears hit the photos,
Huge, hard, miserable tears,
Those were the days,
Those were the days . . .

Emma Bromwich (11)
Invicta Grammar School

MONSTERS IN THE HALLWAY

Monsters in the hallway,
Monsters in your bed,
Monsters everywhere,
Especially in my head.

As I lay in bed at night,
Pictures give me such a fright,
For all around I can see,
Monsters chasing after me.

I lay really still, I pretend I am dead,
Then a bright idea comes into my head,
What if I chanted my special song,
Would the monsters stay away for long?

I decided to chant this special song,
Plum jam, doughnuts, bing bang bong,
Now I feel safe, the monsters have gone,
I hope they will stay away for long.

Claire Holland (13)
Invicta Grammar School

THE DOLPHIN

There I saw it in the sea,
Lying in wait for food.
It moved gracefully,
Hardly disturbing the surface of the still blue water.
As it moved closer I saw the beautiful markings
On its forehead, which glistened in the moonlight.
There it was the mystical and magical dolphin.

Anneka Welstead (12)
Invicta Grammar School

CONFLICT

Cry yourself to sleep at night,
Days are getting longer.
Can you keep it up much more,
Their actions getting stronger?

The energy's seeping out of you,
They have the sense of power.
You have to face them every day,
You see them every hour.

At last the end is near,
You know that they have won.
You feel victory around you,
You couldn't beat the fear.

Clare Ovenden (13)
Invicta Grammar School

THE DEEP BLUE SEA

As the tide whips in and out,
I see the sea's mood change,
In summer it froths and foams,
But in winter it's not the same.

The sea turns into a demon,
Screaming as it hits the rocks,
It's like my wildest dreams,
The waves disappear and disperse.

I can tell the sea my troubles,
As I sit and dream away,
I can see their reflection,
In the crystal diamond glow.

Alexandra Logue (13)
Invicta Grammar School

THE MONSTERS

The monsters came from under the bed,
While the little boy bumped his head.
The monsters didn't realise, what was going on,
So they jumped in front of the boy with a song.
So they sang:- Hello boy what's your name?
    We're the monsters from your game.
    We'd like to know why you've gone red?
    The little boy said, 'I've bumped my head!'
The monsters stood still for a while,
The little boy cried and cried.
The monsters stared crying too,
And then the boy shouted, 'You!'
And pointed his fingers at the yellow one,
'You wimp,' he said, 'what have you done?'
The yellow monster started grinning,
And then shouted 'You are winning!'
The little boy didn't know what he meant,
Until the monster went back under the bed.

Holly Jacobs (13)
Invicta Grammar School

DEATH

So dark and dreary, solemn and still.
So draining, so spiteful.
It feels as though there's nothing left,
Nothing left to feel.
Not anger, frustration, sadness or hate.
Just emptiness, nothing else.

Danielle Hayon (13)
Invicta Grammar School

ALL ALONE

I was playing hide-and-seek,
Hiding out in an old shed.
I sat down, there was a click behind me,
Oh no! The door had shut and locked.

I was in the gloomy old shed,
Somewhere in the middle of the woods.
It felt like I had been here for hours,
No friends and no food.
I felt so helpless, no way I could get out.
I was imagining what freedom was like.
I couldn't help thinking that I was
trapped like a lion in a cage.

The torture is immense,
I am frightened with no one to help me.
I am worried. What if I don't see light again?
Please someone, help!

Emma Smith (13)
Invicta Grammar School

BEATEN

Life can't stop,
life can't end.
I've got a life to lead,
and a life to defend.
I am entitled to lead my own life,
not to be dragged or beaten in the night.

Lauren Cornwall (13)
Invicta Grammar School

BONFIRE NIGHT

Bonfires flaring in the night sky,
On the fire there sits a guy.
Now it is that time of year,
Fireworks going off, don't go near.
In the house, Mum's reading a book,
Raw food on the table, ready for the cook.
Every year this is done, come see the fireworks, look!

Nan's in the house, helping Mum,
I see my sister looking glum.
Go and look into the sky,
Higher and higher the rockets fly,
Time to go now, fireworks finished,
See you next year, bye!

Sam Wiltshire (12)
Invicta Grammar School

IF I WAS . . .

If I was a bird I'd fly high in the sky,
Away from the hatred and people who lie.

If I was a cloud I'd fly high in the air,
Away from the sorrow and the despair.

This world is not happy,
This world is not sweet,
It is full of the sad criticising the meek.

If I was a spirit I'd fly high into heaven,
For what we have done cannot be forgiven.

Hannah Whiteley (13)
Invicta Grammar School

CONFLICT

He was there,
So was I,
He looked at me,
His look was sly.
I stepped forward,
He backed away,
I knew it was going to be,
A tiresome day.
People shouted,
People cheered,
People smiled,
And people jeered.
He threw his first punch,
But hit the air,
Some people laughed,
But he didn't care.
He tried again,
And hit my eye,
I wouldn't give up,
I wouldn't cry.
I returned the punch,
I returned the pain,
I kept on returning,
Again and again.
Then he got mad,
And grabbed my shirt,
We got in a bundle,
Amongst the dirt.
There was kicking and screaming,
And pulling of hair,
Then everyone joined in,
It just wasn't fair.

Then a grown-up voice bellowed,
And everyone ran,
It was the head teacher,
Mr McVan.
We were sent home,
For the rest of the day,
When we told our parents,
They had a lot to say.
I was dying for revenge,
As alone I sat,
But I knew it wasn't worth it,
So I left it at that.

Kate Bourner (13)
Invicta Grammar School

MY WINDOW

I look out of my window,
What do I see?
I see a flower,
The flower of me.

I look out of my window,
What do I see?
I see a rainbow,
With the colours of me.

I look out of my window,
What do I see?
I see a swallow,
With the freedom of me.

I look out of my window,
My life looks back.

Samantha Ayling (12)
Invicta Grammar School

TRAPPED

As soon as I did it,
I wished I hadn't,
Now I've got a record,
I'm stuck in this job,
With no hope of escape,
Stacking shelves full of beans,
Or checking food through the till.

Someone has to help me,
Will I ever be free
From the lingering smell of cheddar and Brie,
From whining kids,
To adults with rage,
They knock everything over,
With not a thought for me.

Yes, I clear it up,
Covered in beans and Brie.

Marissa Mackie (14)
Invicta Grammar School

THE EARTH'S SKY

When I look into the sky I can see,
Gentle white waves on a clear blue ocean.
When you look into the sky you can see,
A million diamonds on a black velvet sheet.
When we look into the sky we can see,
       Our memories.

Rebecca Rank (12)
Invicta Grammar School

SAY GOODNIGHT

The empty church around me,
The atmosphere peaceful and calm,
Lit candles are shining everywhere,
But mostly by the statue of Mary.

I'm leaning on a cold knee rest,
An extra jumper to keep me warm,
In one of the rows of pews,
I am here on my own.

I pray that she'll come back,
One day or another,
I'll be frightened to live without her,
I wouldn't know what to do.

I suppose she can't come back,
She is buried deep underground,
God can't save her now,
He has too many things on his mind.

I will have to say goodnight then,
He can't bring her back,
No matter how almighty he is,
She has gone this time forever.

Joella Webber (12)
Invicta Grammar School

SKIPPY

I have a Chinchilla called Skippy,
Who runs around, and is nippy.
He sleeps all day, and is out of our way,
But wakes up at night to play.

When Skippy comes out to play,
He thinks in his mind, *'Hooray!'*
He chews on cables and legs of tables,
And even the occasional toe.

When Skippy is caught and put in his cage,
He runs around and barks in a rage.
We change his water and give him fresh food,
Turn off the light and leave him in a mood.

He gets me back when I'm in bed,
He jumps around, sounds run through my head.
He bangs and barks like he's swearing at me,
'Please save me from my pet, *Skippy!'*

Samantha-Jane Stopes (13)
Invicta Grammar School

ALONE

In the stillness where the spirit walks,
Is the cool, calm room I'm in,
A room still and dead,
No one talks,
Strong words run through my head,
My heart is still, alone and dead,
Frightened and afraid.

Vittoria Gubbins (12)
Invicta Grammar School

TOO MUCH WORK!

Physics, maths, biology,
English, gym, psychology.
All this work, all this sweat,
I haven't finished my homework yet!

Time for telly, time for tea,
Too much work is bad for me!
Off I go and fall in bed,
Tables and algebra running through my head!

Up at seven, eat at eight,
Hurry up I'm going to be late!
Now I'm in school to learn a new load,
Give me five minutes and my head'll explode!

Rachel Gunstone (12)
Invicta Grammar School

THE LION'S DEN

The lion paced up and down in his cage,
Getting impatient and full of rage,
He was confused, desperate and feeling alone,
His escape seemed to be unknown.

He looked longingly, at the guard asleep on his chair,
The poor lion, he was close to despair,
Then the guard awoke, and to the cage with food, returned,
The lion was angry, the pupil of his eye burned,
To see the creature, that put the lion inside the cage,
Filled the lion's heart with even more rage.

Laura Abbey (13)
Invicta Grammar School

THE 31ST OF OCTOBER

Every single year,
On one certain night,
At the end of October,
You're in for a fright.

The pumpkins are carved,
And the costumes are on,
The night is colder,
Now that summer is gone.

Young children are out,
Their baskets still empty,
By the end of the night,
They'll have sweets a-plenty.

The witches are flying,
And the ghosts are out,
Skeletons rattling,
Lighted pumpkins about.

Spooky music blares,
From discos still going,
Kids are having great fun,
But tiredness is showing.

Though the night's at an end,
It's one we'll remember,
The fun's not over,
Till the fifth of November!

Lizzie Sandon (12)
Invicta Grammar School

BIRTHDAYS!

Birthdays only come,
Once every year.
When my birthday comes around,
I never shed a tear.

I always wake up early,
On the arrival of this day.
I go to unwrap my presents,
Which are stacked in a special kind of way.

The presents are on the bottom,
The cards are on the top.
Some cards fall off the pile,
They land on the floor with a plop.

This year I opened them quickly,
To see what was inside.
I had such a fright,
That I nearly died.

I said, 'Wow, that's amazing,
It's just what I need.'
A little puppy dog,
Of my favourite breed.

My 13th birthday's over,
Another year has passed.
Now comes the 'thank you' letters,
I should start writing fast.

I have so many to write,
They are driving me mad.
Because this year is almost over,
I feel so very sad.

Charlotte Butteriss (13)
Invicta Grammar School

MONSTERS

Last night I saw a monster,
Wandering around my room,
Tearing apart my teddy bears,
And cuddling my mum's broom.

I asked him what he was doing,
He said he was looking for his friend,
They were having a game of hide and seek,
And began to look under the bed.

I said I hadn't seen one,
And told him to go away,
I rolled over to go to sleep,
He was still there the next day.

I took him to school with me,
I got plenty of weird looks,
The teacher wasn't too pleased though,
When he tore up all the books.

She kicked us both out of the school,
We started our way to my house,
Then he began to run away,
He was scared of a little mouse.

That night when I got home,
I went straight to bed,
I was woken by a loud bang,
'Oh no, a monster,' I said.

Emma Berwick (13)
Invicta Grammar School

LET'S GO BOWLING

My daddy took us bowling,
The newest place in town.
He thinks he's a sporting genius,
But he's really a bit of a clown!

We finally arrived there,
Excited as can be.
My dad, my brother and I,
Altogether that makes three!

We put on our special shoes,
And went to find our lane.
I picked up a purple bowling ball,
And then began the game!

I dropped the ball on my big bro's toe,
He screamed and yelped in pain.
I laughed, 'It couldn't hurt that much,
You're just potty and insane!'

We've now finished the bowling game,
And I happened to come last.
It really wasn't fair, you see,
Since, my left arm's in a cast!

Sophie Dewhirst (13)
Invicta Grammar School

MONSTERS

Monsters all around me,
Everywhere I look.
My pencil case, my fountain pen,
Even my science book.

Outer space is where they're from,
Some place we've never heard of.
Living in the far away place,
Known as the planet Zog.

Never returning to this place,
Staying here forever.
We'll probably fight and kill each other,
And be at war together.

So getting back to the original point,
I walked out of my room.
Going down the stairs I think,
'Oh my God, we're doomed.'

To my surprise, they get out the ship,
And walked over to me.
'Greetings Earthling' I hear them say,
'We come here in peace.'

Every monster looks at me,
Like I'm some sort of hope.
And announces they are hungry,
Then produces a bar of soap.

Really excited by this,
I ask for a ride in their ship.
'Of course' says one, 'Why not says another,'
And whisks me away in this.

'So this is how we get craters,'
I say as we hit the moon.
Then a bright light flashes in my eyes,
And I'm back in my bedroom.

Billie-Jo Walters (12)
Invicta Grammar School

FREEDOM

I'm swooping high above the world
As content as the swaying trees,
I think by myself,
I'm self-sufficient
I can come and go as I please.

I have the opportunity to explore
To explore the unknown,
Go to countries where it is hot,
To become relaxed and daring
I'm free.

I am overjoyed to be free,
I can attack birds of prey
Without persecution,
I'm free
I'm a free bird.

Sarah Field (13)
Invicta Grammar School

A MOTHER'S TORMENT

What kind of love is so perpetual?
To compel a vixen to mar her cub.
The mother's torment is so emotional,
She needs to shatter the eternal nub.
The infant arose wailing and howling,
Whilst pa and mama were soundly sleeping.
The putrid smell was overpowering,
The infant in the corner weeping.
Not so long ago that infant was born,
Into his mother's arms he was laid.
Nobody thought they would begin to mourn,
Not even twelve hours on that very same day.
Only the mother knew what was wrong,
She sadly knew that her infant had gone.

Jessica Middleton (15)
Invicta Grammar School

MAZE

I regretted from the moment I walked in,
I knew I would never walk out,
Continually turning, swerving and weaving,
I'm trapped, I can never be free.

Each step I take, another regret,
The world I belonged to has gone,
I'm like an animal trapped in a cage,
I'm desperate, I'm crazy, insane!

Unable to escape, I wander on,
I'm a person trapped in a mind,
Feelings of hunger, thirst and pain,
They exist no longer in me.

As I wonder why I am here,
I see there a small ray of light,
A door, an opening into the world,
Out of the never-ending night.

Claire Pollitt (13)
Invicta Grammar School

To The Sun

You swim the depths of the sea in the sky
A golden majestic ship from the east
I watch in great awe as you sail on by
For as long as you've been, you've never ceased
You are the heaven's life giving angle
You own the day and to us that you give
The gift of creation is your great ball
I thank you for allowing me to live
And no fear have I that you will leave me
For the time of death is merely a taunt
We are bound to each other, never free
For earth is to be your eternal haunt
I am amazed at the work you have done,
Our being, our life is from you dear sun.

Christina Relf (15)
Invicta Grammar School

SCHOOL

I get up at seven
And look out the window,
Then go to the bathroom
And make my hair even.

I get dressed for school
Make my packed lunch,
Then meet up with Barney
And the rest of the bunch.

We race to our lessons
Music, it's boring,
Next we've got English
And outside it's pouring.

At last we have break time
With hot crusty buns,
All smothered in icing
We all say *'Yum, yum!'*

Another two lessons
Art and PE,
As usual exciting
I'm lying - honestly.

It's lunchtime next
Hot eggs and chips,
Maybe a cake
(Or should I say bricks!)

Then last it's physics
The worst of them all,
Five minutes to go
The end of school!

Rachael Nicholson (13)
Invicta Grammar School

WHAT SHALL I DO?

What shall I do when you are no longer here?
You were the tower of strength in my life
The one I turned to when my life was filled with fear
You always helped me when I was in strife
Never moaning but giving good advice
Life would be a shadow, empty and dark
If you weren't close by loving and wise
Life would be a field barren and stark
When you are gone and no longer mine
Tears will be cried but I know that you'll be near
Watching over me our souls combined
Our love for each other will last the years
Life without you will be filled with woe
What that will feel like I do not know.

Hannah Tatton (14)
Invicta Grammar School

HOSTAGE

Nowhere to hide,
As they fire shots at the coach I'm on.
Nowhere to run,
As they take me away towards the desert.
No escape,
As they lock me up and threaten me.
Nothing to do,
As I'm left sitting there waiting to be freed.
No hope,
I'm just a British citizen and want to go home.

Lucy Beazer (13)
Invicta Grammar School

TRAPPED IN THE ATTIC

I creep into the cold attic,
No one will find me here,
I take out a sweet from my pocket,
It tastes full of flavour and tingles
inside my mouth.

The room is dark and still,
My sweets have all gone, now I feel ill.
I have been here so long and have still
not been found.
I can't even hear my friends looking around.
I hear the key slowly turn in the lock and
then I realise I'm trapped!
I feel tricked and start to panic.
I'm scared as I'm now all alone,
I can do nothing, I will wait in the corner
as a helpless heap.
My shouts cannot be heard.
I feel small, lost and frightened.
Now I'm fed-up and want to escape,
I want to be free, as free as a bird
and to live once more.

Jemma Baines (14)
Invicta Grammar School

HALLOWE'EN

Screams and cries everywhere you turn,
Candles inside pumpkins melt and burn.

Children knocking on doors saying 'Trick or treat,'
But all they really want is a nice tasty sweet.

Almost real costumes and brightly coloured hair,
Walk alone through a graveyard if you dare!

The clock strikes midnight, that's it for another year,
When everyone gets home they put away their ghostly gear!

Jessica Duncan (11)
Invicta Grammar School

TRAPPED

As I am walking down the street
I can move my hands, my arms, my feet
My body is free and moves about
But something is stuck and can't get out.
My head is full, jam-packed with woes
Tales of fighting, darkness and foes.
From the outside I look like the rest
Covering up is what I do best.
It can't get out. It can't escape.
It haunts me when I am awake.
It keeps me from the Land of Nod
Every day I pray to God
I want to be released from fear
I want the hole to disappear
Why do people rush about?
They're so free - I want to shout.
'Stop' to the world 'Wait for me'
I am trapped in a fantasy.
Why can't I move? Why am I stuck?
I want my head set free from muck.
So think of me if you can
For I am trapped in my fantasy land.

Emma Hollamby (13)
Invicta Grammar School

BEING TRAPPED

As I sat in my cage looking out into the big wide world,
all I could see were birds flying . . .
. . . *free.*
I felt alone and imprisoned by these four wooden walls
towering around me.
I felt as if I was a mouse being chased by a raging lion.
Then suddenly one of the four wooden walls opened
and in came a large hairy pink hand.
As the hand lowered I became petrified and my face
started to shiver and a fearful look came over me . . . then,
Whoosh! I was free. I was free to roam anywhere.
I was carried two metres to a box of wire.
In the box there were long lushes of green grass
that looked very appetising.
I was placed in the box and was now free to explore
my new bigger world that was full of life.

Laura Crump (13)
Invicta Grammar School

THE POND

The pond was in the countryside, quiet and still.
The mud swirling round and round,
              will settle on the cold damp ground.
The mole looked in the pond and saw the sun,
A dragon saw a battle in which he won.
The hare looked in the pond and saw a running race,
A tortoise had a look and saw a faster pace.
The fox looked in the pond and saw a place to play,
A homeless deer had a look and saw a place to stay.
The herd of cattle looked in the pond and saw a green field,
A farmer glanced in one day, the secrets of the pond revealed.

Annie Biddlecombe (12)
Invicta Grammar School

As Free As Bird

Imagine yourself as a bird,
Flying high and free above the trees,
Travelling miles every day,
Visiting houses and buildings where lots of children play,
This is what it is like to be as free as a bird.

Imagine yourself as a bird,
With lots of space and blue sky to roam,
Leaving your nest when you like,
Not worrying when to go home.

Imagine yourself as a bird,
Having fun, flying around with lots of independence,
Very excited about my adventures each day.
With lots of energy . . . *I can never be sad.*

Nina Hicks (14)
Invicta Grammar School

Deep Pan Pizza

Under the deep pan crust of the earth like a stuffed pizza,
Hot, bubbling molten rock waits apprehensive and agitated,
While a topping full of exciting activities is carrying on with
its life on the surface.
This topping trapped the molten rock which lies beneath the
deep pan crust of the earth.
The molten rock feels trapped in the hot temperatures beneath.
The topping of buildings, cars and people is free in the cool air.
The molten rock is wishing that the pressure could escape,
Like a pressure cooker steaming on the hot flame,
But it must wait for the right moment to catch this busy world
of topping by surprise.

Sophie Byfield (13)
Invicta Grammar School

NIGHT TRAPS

Out of breath,
Running in everlasting circles,
Round and round the strange building,
Eyes everywhere,
Through the gloom,
Tapping into my brain,
Wicked laughing echoes around.

The devil appears,
With a fork in his hand,
Not a devil,
A dragon,
Charging at me,
Breathing flames and laughing.

An earthquake,
A red light,
Flames,
The devil raised on a platform,
Rising through the roof,
The roof falls onto me,
Another earthquake begins.

I grasp the side of the bed in terror,
The earthquake carries on,
So does my nightmare.

Claire Brown (13)
Invicta Grammar School

THE HOSTAGE

Free as a bird,
Free as the wind,
Free to do as I please.

Filled with joy and relief,
Time to talk and sing and dance.

My thoughts of never seeing my
family again are gone once more.

I know how much I have changed,
So I wonder whether I will recognise them.

Who are these people walking towards me?
Is it them?
I do not know.

They look familiar
Are they the same?
How will I ever know?

I pass them by,
I give them a loving gaze.

They didn't even notice me.
I feel so wounded and anger fills my heart.

At last I am free . . .

Emma Ballard (13)
Invicta Grammar School

CHILD ABUSE

The anxiety of waiting,
The tense nervous headaches,
When will I be free
From this terrible place?
Warm and cosy,
Yes it may be,
But still doesn't look after me.

They batter, they bruise me
Chat about me, accuse me.
Even though I've done nothing wrong.

My only crime is to live and breathe,
And maybe sing a heart-warming song.

A few years to go,
Then maybe I'll be,
Free as a bird,
No worries for me.

Amie Woodward (13)
Invicta Grammar School

MY FAT PONY

His name was Mr Greedy,
He was short, fat and round,
He was never very speedy,
Because his belly touched the ground.
Me and Mr Greedy,
Were pals ever after,
Me and Mr Greedy,
He fills my life with laughter.

Laura Yeo (13)
Invicta Grammar School

THE INVISIBLE BOX

I'm trapped
in my own fragile box,
it has no walls, no roof, no floor,
but I can't get out, however I may try.
No sunlight can penetrate through,
no birds can I hear singing,
I can't remember my parents' faces,
nor remember their soothing words.
All I can feel are these cold hands,
transporting me at their will.
I have no say, no wage, nor pay,
for going through this pain.
I pray every night from my bed,
but God never hears my pledge.
I pray one day I may see my parents,
and tumble and roll with my dad,
but for a while I have to picture the fun
we would have from memory.
I'm always alone,
so terribly alone.
I am my only friend.
The doctors say there is no hope,
no way I can get out.
I'm just one in a number of children,
who are deaf,
who are blind,
who are dumb.

Kelly Stephenson (13)
Invicta Grammar School

SPACE: THE FINAL FRONTIER

The universe, a never-ending place
Lots of planets orbiting here and there
And millions of stars floating in space
It is gobsmacking and will make you stare
Comets and asteroids whizzing about
Black holes, stars and red - dwarfs are always near
The man in the moon is just coming out
As you fly through space, there's nothing to fear
Travelling swiftly, the final frontier
Maybe there is a stop to the universe
Stars and planets are becoming clearer
Like a story, a poem or a verse
The music of space just keeps going on
Space: the final frontier, a spaceman's song.

Laura Hollamby (14)
Invicta Grammar School

VOLCANO

Trapped, I bubble and boil alone,
Trapped, swirling round without taking any form,
Trapped, a semi-solid structure, sloshing around,
Swirling melted rock. I flow round and round, below
The gust in an inferno of heat.

Trapped, I can't get free, I'm losing hope after
being here millions of years. Trapped!
Trapped, but I can see a crack, I wait for
the right moment, then I burst out.
Yippee! I'm out, I'm free.

I flow down the hills, burning all in my path,
bubbling as I roll down. But the cold reaches my centre,
I slow down to a halt, I can't move.
Solid, I feel the molten rock below me trying to burst out.
Now I'm the crust. Trapped!

Michelle Turner (14)
Invicta Grammar School

BOXED BEAR

I'm an unwanted bear,
With nothing new to see,
But the four cardboard walls,
That have forever confined me.

I've felt the same old feelings,
Of rejection and desperation.
I've felt like a rat trapped in a cave,
I've felt the suffocation.

I've been in this box for years,
Looking at nothing new.
I've seen these four cardboard walls,
I know them through and through.

I sit here doing nothing,
But twiddling my matted fur thumbs.
I pray and fool myself,
Hoping that someone comes.

Gemma Cornford (13)
Invicta Grammar School

TRAPPED IN A BOX

I am a bear.
Shiny red nose,
Buttons for eyes,
And a blue bow tie.
I have been trapped in a box in the loft,
I am loved no more,
I am just too old.
I have a light bulb as my light source,
Otherwise, complete darkness.

Lots of bustling down below,
What's going on? I ask,
A light before me appeared,
Then a shadow covered it,
It was like a cloud covering the sun,
The lid on my box closed,
I feel scared, alone, angry, frightened.
I want to get out.
          Bang!
Where am I? I ask myself.
I was in the box for some time,
I didn't like the darkness,
It shocked me when the box lid opened,
The light from the sun blinded me,
I was laid on the floor,
I feel free as a bird.

Humans walk past,
Take a look at me then walk on,
The day passes,
Back I go into that same old box,
Trapped once more.

Jenni Baldwin (13)
Invicta Grammar School

HEAVEN

Heaven is a place we don't know about,
Stories are told about heaven and hope,
We all want to go there when time is out,
The idea of this place helps us cope.
Love is like heaven helping us through,
It seems so much easier with a dream,
I know I love my life, just me and you,
My memories of us make my day gleam.
I often think about one another,
Will our love last through it, thick and thin?
Could we really live without each other?
Sometimes I feel you're my next of kin.
Heaven is there for us all at a date,
Heaven is love and for you I will wait.

Beth Tayler (14)
Invicta Grammar School

BLIND

I listen for a sound,
A whisper,
How I long to see the sunshine,
To see my family,
I'm alone,
Who can I turn to?
No one understands,
All the colours of the rainbow I can't see,
It's so frustrating,
So many things going through my mind,
All that tells me I'm blind.

Laura Boucher (11)
Invicta Grammar School

THE DEEP BLUE OCEAN

The sea is a totally different world,
A deep blue ocean full of mysteries,
Deep, deep down where the white coral is curled,
It does have many creepy histories,
Where great big ferry boats glide overhead,
And the dolphins follow closely behind,
It could act like it is nearly dead,
Being very calm, it almost seems kind,
Under the waves, colourful fish do roam,
Blue, yellow, silver, red, all these shining,
Big waves rise and then fall leaving a foam,
The waves reach great height and then start falling,
The wide ocean blue, a wonderful thing,
About the ocean the sea birds do sing.

Rachel Whitehead (14)
Invicta Grammar School

POVERTY

Working our way through the dark grim streets,
Cheerlessness and depression surrounds us,
People lie on mats and stare up at us,
Their eyes filled with misery, wretchedness and despair.

They lie defenceless, powerless and weak.
Their bodies so thin
Sickness is rife
I see dying everywhere.

My stomach churns as I see the conditions.
I feel powerless to act.
My lamplight creeps over these abandoned people.
These are people trapped in poverty.
These are people the world forgot.

Nicola Crozier (13)
Invicta Grammar School

ETERNAL LOVE

Oh why are you not standing here with me?
Why did you have to leave me here alone?
I recall the times we'd share by the sea
Now - just memories, I sit here at home.
The day you left me, I'll never forget.
I lie here in torment and slowly die.
Addicted to work - what a wonderful vet
But so many times you used to tell lies.
Oh I will never, ever forget you
You have been a major part of my life
Someone will replace you - I know, but who?
I know he won't give me half as much strife
I thought that our love would be eternal
It was just going through a long dark tunnel.

Diana Merwood (14)
Invicta Grammar School

What Is To Become?

Was this the end of this wondrous day?
The sea seemed to turn a glittering blue,
You drifted away and left me to pay.
What was left was nothing, only I knew.
I floated along the long distant shore,
Everything was drawing, quite so near.
What was to become was so unsure,
I have lost the one that I love so dear.
Will I ever come back to this place,
Was it him or me that drifted apart?
He could find me one day without a trace.
If he doesn't believe take both our hearts,
I saw him appear so quick, like a dove,
Together at last, so in love.

Rebecca Brooker (14)
Invicta Grammar School

Lululapoe

There is a place where warm winds do blow,
And the air is filled with a sweet perfume,
Along the banks of the Lululapoe,
The Violama bird sings her soft tune.

Deep in the rushes the Stookabray sleeps,
After a long day this weary beast rests,
None can discover the secrets she keeps,
Tucked away safely beneath her warm breast.

For she is the last left here of her kind,
Alone by the lake in Lululapoe,
The birth of her pups is very well timed,
As the years on her now begin to show.

Life will go on in the land time can't reach,
The waters will run on into the breach.

Laura Williams (15)
Invicta Grammar School

ALONG DEATH'S PATH

Drifting though a sea of time is our love,
Our feelings, so strong they will never part,
Our love, purer than the wings of a dove,
You are my soul and the life in my heart.
Although we fall apart it never lasts,
We can't get by without one another,
I adore you, don't think about the past,
We don't need that now we have each other.
Don't worry about fate, we can get by,
No harm will come to us if you believe,
Our bond is so tight, our love will not die,
Together forever I will not grieve.
We can die together when the time is right,
When the stars are out in the dead of night.

Carly Ambrose (14)
Invicta Grammar School

A LOVE TRUE AND DEEP

Pierced straight through the heart by Cupid's arrow,
Darting swiftly through the sky down to you,
Long golden and the end sharp and narrow.
Splitting the soft white milky clouds in two.
As the arrow hit, magic could be seen,
A glow so bright that the world stood quite still,
A feeling as though the angels had just been.
Your eyes lit with a certain sparkling will.
We came closely together hand in hand,
Felt between us was a love true and deep,
And for eternity forever we stand.
A love that could fill an ocean we could keep,
So if we feel the same in our hearts,
Then let us never ever be apart.

Nicola Fitz-Gerald (15)
Invicta Grammar School

ME!

The writer of this poem,
Has hair golden like the sun,
As beautiful as a sunset,
Like a cheetah when she runs.

As rosy as a red apple,
As clumsy as a bull,
As brainy as a dictionary,
Like a magnet when she pulls.

As mad as a mad hatter,
As quick as a lightning flash,
As strong as a heavy weight,
As scary as a thunder crash.

The writer of this poem,
Sounds just like you,
This could all be a lot of nonsense,
No one said it had to be true!

Vicky Ansty (13)
Invicta Grammar School

IS THIS LOVE?

Is this love I feel deep inside my heart?
This emotion I feel I can't hide.
Sensations I felt for you from the start,
A feeling no precious jewels can provide.
Your looks struck me like Cupid's arrow,
I was blinded by your gorgeous blue eyes.
You are the heavens of which I stand below,
Looking up at your beauty as it shines.
When I am with you, my heart starts to race,
Because of the joy you send to my heart.
I feel I am in the most blessed place
And from you I could never bear to part.
So is this love I feel inside my heart?
And will you be struck with Cupid's love dart?

Natasha Spencer (14)
Invicta Grammar School

TOGETHERNESS

Plunging pendulums are perpetual,
As I fall deeper from contentment mine,
But as I feel your warmth come over all,
Tepid joy rids me of my painful pine.
The twinge of bashfulness slips from my glee,
Shafts of anxiety fall from my bliss,
Leaving me to relish in praise of thee,
And now angelic rays do shine from this.
Ecstasy shocks and astonishes us,
Together we rest in carpeted love,
Woe is translucent as we mix in lust,
We are blessed by angels from skies above.
Close proximity enhances elation,
We grow together as one creation.

Rachel Gardner (14)
Invicta Grammar School

ODE TO GARLIC

Garlic, garlic everywhere.
Feed it to your teddy bear,
Put it on your toast and bread,
Think about it in your head.
Listen up and listen well,
Garlic, garlic, what a smell!

Jenni Hardes (13)
Invicta Grammar School

LEOPARD

Stealthily sliding across a survivor's safari
Lapping up a gentle breeze which whispers at its side
The glare of the sun shooting over its back
But slow to keep up with its swift race
A race against time, against illusions of justice.

The shadows creep along its dusty path
Treading at its menace
Feeling the heartbeat of its prey,
Wallowing in fear as the creature stands poised.
Silence but audible!
A cry out but not enough time
Life but death!

The leopard crashes into its prey
Teeth plunging into its flesh,
Tearing it to shreds and leaving it shattered
in a thousand pieces
Left to die, curled up like the rolling tide of an ocean,
Rippled with pain.

The cruel ebony black eyes riddled with pleasure,
A shadow drawn across them creating a fearsome darkness.
Body scarred with a pale spectrum of light
and splashes of colour
Its beauty surpasses the guilt
Its prey is left, strewn across the bloody grass and
the leopard creeps away . . . *slowly* . . . *slowly* . . . *slowly* . . .

Erin Dodds (13)
Invicta Grammar School

OH FOR A CAT

Oh for a cat with a very long tail,
And eyes as bright as the stars,
Who goes out all night to chase all the mice,
And only returns at dawn.

Oh for a cat with a very sleek body,
Who could creep through the tiniest crack,
And could balance on the narrowest rail or ledge,
And even play notes on my piano.

Oh for a cat, who could hear every word, that you
say in the day and the night,
And always frighten burglars away,
By swishing his tail and showing his teeth,
And be proud of the job he has done.

Oh for a cat who would lay by the fire, at night, when
it's cold in the winter,
And always come back so we know he is safe and
never stays out all night,
And when he comes in all wet from the rain,
He'll sit by the fire again.

Oh for a cat who would sit very still,
And not break every vase in the house,
Who would never leave holes in the furniture,
And after sleeping in beds, would never leave fur.

Oh for a cat who would never leap out of windows,
Even though we knew he could do it quite safely.
And would never wake us up at five o'clock in the morning,
And purr really loudly so that we could hear him.

And oh for a cat who would always be good,
And never scratch or fight,
And when he comes in from chasing the mice,
Only then will we give him his supper.

Tamara Young (11)
Maidstone Grammar School For Girls

SEASONS

I love spring,
When things turn green,
I love to watch the flowers,
And the bees that go between.

I love summer,
When it's nice and hot,
I join in a water fight,
Carrying water in a pot.

I love autumn,
When leaves turn brown,
I put them in a pile,
Then jump in and knock them down.

I love winter,
I love it when it snows,
We gather round the fire,
Then sit and warm our toes.

I love all the seasons,
I really can't decide,
Whether I like winter when I'm frozen,
Or summer when I'm fried.

Kayley Prebble (13)
Maidstone Grammar School For Girls

BISCUITWRAPPUSCRISPPACKETUS

Have you heard, have you seen?
There's a new flower - it's quite obscene!
It's squarish in shape with torn battered edges,
And it's covered in brown greasy film.

My goodness is there?
It sounds absurd!
What's its name?
I hadn't heard.

It's the Biscuitwrappuscrisppacketus and it really is unique.
They're easy to find and simple to seek,
I come across hundreds each week!
They're impaled on every roadside hedge,
They clog up every drain.
They brighten up the highways and they pitter patter in the rain.

My goodness me!
Oh, haven't you heard?
The world really does have the brain of a bird!

Camilla Egginton (12)
Maidstone Grammar School For Girls

MY INVISIBLE FRIEND

My invisible friend goes wherever I go,
My invisible friend is called Mary.
She goes here, she goes there,
My invisible friend goes everywhere.

Mary comes with me all the time,
Across the stream or down the lane.
I talk to her in the poppy fields,
And she stays inside with me when it rains.

Mary is different to my school friends,
She never argues or is a pain.
She's always there through bad and good,
Mary's a bit shy but we are still friends.

My mum, dad and brother don't believe me,
When I talk about my invisible friend.
They say 'Where is she?' and they never find her,
I say she's with me and we both like to play.

Victoria Rogers (12)
Maidstone Grammar School For Girls

ME

I'm as quick and bright as lightning,
I shine like a diamond ring.
I'm as witty as a comic,
Respected like a King.

I'm as jolly as a Christmas Eve,
As friendly as a postman.
As gentle as a butterfly,
With the might of every ocean.

I truly am the Queen of art,
My work will sell for millions!
I'm as groovy as the top pop star.
My fans? Well I've got billions.

It must be said, I shall admit,
That perfect I cannot be.
I have one fault, a minor fault,
I'm far too modest, me.

Laura Kerr (13)
Maidstone Grammar School For Girls

MY SECRET NIGHTMARES

It had come to the end of a busy day,
The night was drawing nearer.
I peacefully lay inside my bed,
So all my thoughts came clearer.

It was then beneath the duvet cover
When I began to see;
The darkness figures around me hover,
Advancing to capture me:

The tall ones hiding in my cupboard,
The thin ones from in my drawer.
The fat ones lurking behind the sideboard
And many, many more!

It was as if it was a 'ghostie' ball
And me their dancing partner.
Though, they wouldn't dance with me at all,
But eat me as their starter.

What could I do? Should I scream?
Or stay and suffer hell?
If I told you a secret about my dream,
Please could you promise not to tell? . . .
. . . Because . . . I'm afraid of the *dark!*

Helen Thornewell (12)
Maidstone Grammar School For Girls

HOMEWORK

Homework at primary school was always a chore,
I thought it was such an incredible bore,
but now I know it was short and easy
'Cos senior school homework is really sleazy.

Maths, English, history and technology,
Geography, science, French and psychology.
These are only just a few,
Of the pieces of homework we're likely to do.

So I no longer have time to play,
'Cos it's work, work, work every day.

Alex Wright (11)
Norton Knatchbull School

THE STAIRS

On the stairs
Nobody cares
Shoving and pushing
Is anybody looking?
Some boys are big
Some boys are small
But most of all
The boys are oh so tall.
Banging and crashing
Little ones dashing
But I know I'll get there
Stair by stair by stair.

Jean-Philippe Lappage (11)
Norton Knatchbull School

THE TEACHER

In he walked,
Whilst the children fought,
And talked.

They jabbed,
And stabbed,
They behaved quite mad,

'Be quiet' he said,
But no one stirred,
Not one head,

The teacher decided to sit this out,
But more they caused havoc,
And more did they shout,

So without success,
Just like all the rest
The teacher, he left in distress.
Never to come back,

Yes, now they still sit,
Class 7 Barrett,
Unconquered and free,
Come on let's, *party!*

Jack Allen (11)
Norton Knatchbull School

BEHIND THE DOOR

My head spins like a propeller
Rattling in my brain,
I drag my feet along the khaki carpet
Of the gloomy corridor.

I squint as I approach the door.
I tremble like the bells of a tambourine,
As I imagine the tyrannical horror,
Lurking behind the door.

My spine shivers,
As I picture a shrivelled face,
Beckoning me in,
Like a dark spectre,
Lurking behind the door.

The curse is upon me,
The words pound my head like a drum,
Detention, detention,
Lurking behind the door.

My knuckles cripple as I attempt to knock.
The shadow of the wall looms like a fiery dragon.
Its grotesque spirit about to leap out
And tear me apart.

Then I wait,
Blood bubbling in my veins,
Furiously trying to escape me,
Draining my soul.

Then it stops,
Suddenly. The silence breaks.
'Come in,'
A voice utters.

Patrick Williams (11)
Norton Knatchbull School

CLEAN FREAK

My brother sits in the corner of the room,
Holding a duster and a broom,
Whenever he has a little time,
He spends it on getting rid of grime,
Wherever dust and cobwebs lurk,
He beats them all like Captain Kirk,
I once saw him getting rid of a sock,
It gave me such an awful shock,
He kicks them up and treats them rough,
If I was a sock I'd find it tough,
I never have known anyone like him,
Though I think his life must be very dim,
I don't know what I'm going to do because my
Mum's a clean freak too.

Kevin Bennett (11)
Norton Knatchbull School

SCHOOL

I stand at the doors,
Looking up at the school,
Something strange makes me feel so small,
My backpack is bulging I'm ready to go,
All I do now is get in with the flow.

I look around
For people I've known,
But when I see them they seem to have grown.
They're older and wiser it's plain to see,
And I'm pleased to say they're a lot like me.

Joshua Bolton (11)
Norton Knatchbull School

CLASSROOM CHAOS

At lunchtime in the classroom,
Chaos rules for evermore,
Pupils shouting across the room,
And paper all over the floor.

Graffiti on the walls,
Pen marks on the table,
'Oi John, what's the answers to the homework?'
'Lend us your ruler Mabel.'

Then a teacher enters, and complains about the mess,
And also all the noise
And sends most people out of the room,
(It's usually all the boys).

Then we get a *huge* telling off,
And some extra work (a massive, massive pile),
And then the teacher leaves and we are silent . . .
. . . For a while.

William Wraxall (11)
Norton Knatchbull School

MY GRANDAD

My grandad was a famous player.
For ten years he was Luton's best!
He entertained thousands or more.
They all marvelled at his skills.
The home crowd would clap and cheer.
He often played up front.
He was the crowd's favourite player.
After all, he was Luton band's best
                              trumpet player!

Joe Smith (11)
Norton Knatchbull School

THE VILLAGE DRAGON

The charred remains they told their story.
The village street was gaunt and gory.
The skeletal houses,
Structures open to the sky
All because of the village dragon.
He lurked in his cave at the top of the hill.
His scales were musty with age.
The cave was black with soot and smoke,
Which came from his nostrils.
His teeth were blunted by the bones of men
And his breath stank of death and fire,
The old dragon snorted as he lay in his palace,
As he surveyed his blackened kingdom
                              And steamed.

Edward Pont (12)
Norton Knatchbull School

THE AUTUMN DANCE

Leaves rustling in the strong gale,
And friskily jiggling about.
Twigs snapping under my feet,
As sparrows leave for another place.
Conkers rolling past,
Spiky brown and green shells,
Scattered all over the path.
As winter returns,
The autumn colours fade away
Until they come another day.
The snowflakes cover the trees,
With a white, silk coat.

Fredo Hornung (11)
Norton Knatchbull School

GHOST POEM

I walked along the moor one day,
Everywhere was dark and grey,
A whirling wind whooshed me around,
And dropped me down with a thud on the ground,
I walked along to a strange looking home,
It had four large towers and a great murky dome,
I knocked on the knocker which is a bat's face,
The door disappeared without a trace,
I walked into the gloomy room,
The clock struck twelve, the hour of doom,
A gust of wind came through the door,
A howling came from the unknown moor,
Soon the lights blew out in the hall,
A large clear object flew through the wall,
It flew around howling and screaming,
I was so surprised I felt I was dreaming,
It flew towards me and stuck out its arm,
It gave off a smell quite like a farm,
It came close to me and went 'Woo ho,'
'Please be scared it's the best I can do.'
He started to weep, he started to cry,
He then flew away within a blink of an eye.

Michael Trickett (12)
Norton Knatchbull School

THE POSTMAN

I rise at four, it's early you know,
I go in all weathers, wind, rain or snow.
I put on my uniform all smart and neat,
I put on my boots to cover my feet.

I like a good breakfast to start the day,
And after my eggs, I'm on my way.
I start up my car with a whirr and a roar,
I push my foot down, hard to the floor.

I arrive at my workplace all brightly lit,
And see colleagues arriving, looking sprightly and fit.
I go inside to get my bag for the day,
Then set off outside, I'm on my way.

I walk the streets as the sun starts to rise,
I think to myself who will get a surprise.
I walk down street paths, and put things through doors.
If you've not guessed who I am,
I'm the postman, of course.

James Knight (12)
Norton Knatchbull School

OLD JACK BROWN

There was a man called old Jack Brown
Upon his face he wore a frown.
His legs were bent, he had funny feet.
Not the man you would like to meet!

His head was big, his eyes were round,
His old grey coat hung to the ground!
He wore a hat that covered his ears,
And he must have reached at least eighty years.

He had a pointed nose, his hair was grey,
And he'd only come out at the end of the day.
To walk to the end of his lonely old street,
With a terrible limp and a dragging of feet.

He lives in a house with a bright green door,
With a tatty old mat to cover his floor!
Wherever I see him he always looks down!
I feel really sorry for old Jack Brown.

Jamie West (12)
Norton Knatchbull School

TOM IS A BOY OF EXTREME PERSONALITY

His clothes are clean and trimmed not dirty,
His dad has an age of round about thirty!

His hands smell fresh and nice,
Like paprika and pepper spice.

He is not too fat or too thin,
Not like a beachball or a pin.

He goes to church every Sunday,
He goes to school every Monday.

He does his homework every day,
He is always happy for his hair is not grey!

He watches telly in his spare time,
He sits on the sofa with his pet gopher,
Gordon is its name.

Chris Borman (12)
Norton Knatchbull School

THE THING

I can't believe it's happened,
I can't believe it's here,
What I can't say,
But it happened in May,
Sometime this year.

It makes a noise,
It likes to shout,
It wails all night,
Gives the neighbours a fright,
They don't like to hang about.

It likes to poke,
It likes to pick,
It eats so bad,
It makes me mad,
It makes me want to be sick.

I've tried to get rid of it,
I've even asked my mother,
She says, 'Oh no!
This cannot be so!
For he's your baby brother!'

Sam Butler (12)
Norton Knatchbull School

THE SPY

This is the man
that does what he can
to deceive his enemies' plans

He carries a gun
with it, battles he's won
but he doesn't consider it fun

He jumps he crawls
he can climb up walls
he's so sure-footed, he never falls

His clothes are black
useful for an attack
but courage he certainly does not lack

His actions are brave
so hostages can be saved
then his foes will rant and rave

He starts to run
his deeds are done
now he can see his six year old son

At the end of the day
he can cheer 'Hooray'
now he can go and get his pay.

Edward Rummins (12)
Norton Knatchbull School

My Old Uncle Called Tim

I have an old Uncle called Tim
Who is extraordinarily dim
His brain is so small
I'm surprised he's got one at all
And I am ashamed to have a relative like him.

He wears an old pair of jeans
So worn that even the seams
Are so threadbare and worn
That the knees are all torn
It's surprising he's got another pair of trousers,
                                that's how it seems.

His shirt is all dirty and creased
And his hair is all scruffy and greased
He smells of BO
This happens to show
He looks like a savaged beast.

His unshaven beard is all long
And this looks terribly wrong
His nose is all hairy
It looks really scary
And boy oh boy what a pong.

So if you see a scruffy man who is dim
Please be careful with him
If he looks all bony
Not half as fast as a pony
Chances are, it's my uncle called Tim.

Jonathan Salt (12)
Norton Knatchbull School

THINKING IN PARADISE

I am lying here
Hot and sunny
Just lying there on a beach.
As I lie there
The cliffs shadow over me.
I lie there thinking
Just thinking
About life
Good things
Bad things.
As the waves roll over
I think of nothing.
Occasionally the sun hides
Behind a cloud.
A gust of wind whistles through
Bringing the smell and sound
Ever closer to me.
I lie there still
As still as a corpse.

Michael Vargyas (14)
St Anselm's Catholic School, Canterbury

A HORSE

A beautiful stallion roaming free
galloping along the frost-bitten sea
cantering along the crisp green grass
ever wishing it would last
the tail glistened in the morning sunlight
making it shine a shimmering white.

Sam A Murray (11)
St Anselm's Catholic School, Canterbury

CORNFIELD

I am sitting in a cornfield,
I see golden corn glinting in the sun,
I smell the freshly harvested corn,
I hear corn mice scattering all around me,
I taste the fresh country air,
I feel the prickly corn on my skin,
I am happy here and I feel at rest.
But then the sound was broken by noisy traffic,
The smell was broken by car exhaust fumes,
The sight was destroyed by ugly cars and vehicles
                                travelling down a road,
The taste was broken by a speeding motorbike's exhaust fumes,
And I feel uncomfortable because I cannot rest,
I have lost the best.

Lee Phillips (14)
St Anselm's Catholic School, Canterbury

THE HIGHWAY

One hot day
The sun burning my neck
The wind blowing
Into my ears
Birds singing
People talking
Cars driving past
Fumes blowing into my face
The blue bright sky
Catching my eyes
When I look up.

Glenn Phipps (14)
St Anselm's Catholic School, Canterbury

THE TRAPPED TIGER

Why do they stare?
Why don't they care?
Why am I here?
Feeling this fear.

What are those bars?
So cold and hard.
Please let me out,
I want to shout.

My home should be,
In the jungles green,
Not in this place,
With so little space.

I'm stuck in this crate,
And that's not great,
Where are they taking me?
Where will it be?

The shaking and rattling,
Has suddenly stopped,
With a clang and a clank,
The door is dropped.

What can I see?
Is this a dream?
Is it a jungle,
So nice and green?

Can it be true?
Am I now home?
Here in my jungle,
I will always roam.

Antonia Pringle (12)
St Anselm's Catholic School, Canterbury

MY FAVOURITE PLACE

I'm at my favourite place,
Walking along,
Listening to the cold wind whistle
In my ears.

I start to walk a little quicker,
As the rain gets rather thicker,
I listen to it trickling down my coat,
Down my face,
Down my arms.

The grey sky opens up once more,
And the rain falls to the floor,
The wind rustles in my hair,
As I start to stare,
At the roaring waves,
Making my days,
At my favourite place.

Annika Apps (14)
St Anselm's Catholic School, Canterbury

LONDON

In London it is very crowded,
the people shout and argue.
I can feel the breath upon my neck,
the people look like little specks.

There are millions of cars,
the fumes oozing out poison,
which wreaks havoc on the ozone.

Sometimes it smells disgusting,
the sewage and fumes make a deadly
concoction for all that breathe.

London is as hot as hell,
the humidity clogs my lungs.
The air is close enough to strangle a man to death.

Anthony Price (14)
St Anselm's Catholic School, Canterbury

COUNTRYSIDE

I sit and stare,
I watch and learn,
As everything passes by.

The grass is cut,
The lambs are born,
And the clouds are
In the sky.

The sun comes out,
The flowers grow,
People come out
To sit and sew.

The woods are dark,
With stars so bright,
That just keep twinkling
In the night.

Christine Scott (14)
St Anselm's Catholic School, Canterbury

THE SEA

I am near the sea,
I can smell the salt,
hear the waves,
taste the sand
and see young children paddling.

I can feel the hot, gritty sand between my toes,
the sun on my skin,
the sea is very green,
the blue sky is glistening down onto it,
making it glitter.

In the distance I can see fog clouds coming,
now I can feel a chill,
no one else has seemed to notice,
but I have,
I'm going home now.

Kelly Myles (14)
St Anselm's Catholic School, Canterbury

MY TEDDY AND ME

My pink ted called Ned, does nothing all day but
Sit on my bed. He's grubby and lovely and
listens intently to every word that's plainly said.

I think Natalie loves me, maybe not
So much when she was little.
The dolls have gone and make-up
has come along, and I sometimes
wonder will she forget her special ted?

Natalie Meehan (11)
St Anselm's Catholic School, Canterbury

THE BEACH

I sit on the stony beach
Outside my house
No one's around, not even a mouse.
It is so quiet that I can hear the
Waves lap onto the stones.
When it is very hot
I can imagine that I am on a sandy beach.
There are colours of
Grey for the stones,
Blue for the sea,
Green for the seaweed,
Brown for the muddy seabed.

Sarah Goulding (14)
St Anselm's Catholic School, Canterbury

SINGING SOLO

I sing solo in the choir at school,
I love it!
The buzz when you know people are there to see you;
The great feeling of the applause you get;
The song meaning nothing but also everything;
The achievement of finishing;
The eyes that fix upon you;
The feeling of happiness that makes you excited;
The feeling of fear that goes on with you but then disappears;
The praise you get from teachers, parents and friends;
The song that stays in your head.

Rachel Albrecht (14)
St Anselm's Catholic School, Canterbury

The Owl

There is an owl perched
in a tree.
Who always does
stare straight at me.
If I look in his eyes
what on earth
would I see?
Is it as black as
the night?
Or is it as bright as
a light?
But does he have
a soul like
me?

Ricky Wincote (14)
St Anselm's Catholic School, Canterbury

Sea!

As you hear the waves
Crashing, banging on the rocks
Watch the wind
Brush over the sea
You can feel the sand
Brushing through your feet
And taste the salt
In the sea
And smell
The fresh sea breeze
Combining all these senses
You can find life!

Sabrina Coupland (14)
St Anselm's Catholic School, Canterbury

FREEDOM

Who is that handsome tiger in that cage?
Look at his eyes and the way he walks
I wish he could be free just like me

Every day he goes to the ring to do daring tricks
Like jumping through fire rings
And making tiger pyramids
Why don't they let him go?

I look at the keeper feeding him every day
I wish one day he would let him go away

And then one day the keeper feeds him
But forgets to lock the door
It takes a minute for him to realise
But when he does he's away like a flash.

Ben Swinfield (13)
St Anselm's Catholic School, Canterbury

MY HOLIDAY

I'm so excited,
Waiting to get on the aeroplane,
Everybody trying to get to their seats,
The plane seems so crowded,
And small,
Waiting to take off,
To get to the sunny island,
People sitting so still,
Looking so nervous.
I just want to get there,
In the warm weather
And soon I will be.

Victoria Newport (14)
St Anselm's Catholic School, Canterbury

THE BEACH

As I sit along the sea shore
Hearing the big waves roar

The bright sun beaming down on me
Makes me want to run in

Seeing boats come in then out
See surfers all about

As I walk along the sea shore
My feet sink in the golden sand
And the gentle sea breeze
Blows on my face

I can see the brightly coloured buoy
Bobbing up and down
Really far out

I wonder what's hanging about out there.

Victoria Bounds (14)
St Anselm's Catholic School, Canterbury

ROGER

Roger my teddy is fluffy
He has a very long tail
He wears rainbow-coloured trousers
That come down to his knees
He sticks out his tongue which is red as a rose
He has Dumbo ears to shut out the noise
I sat Roger on my bed by my pillow
He sits there still today.

I like it when Charlotte snuggles up to me
On freezing cold winter nights
I sit on her pillow with other toys
Placed neatly in a row
On hot summer nights I end up on the floor
Because Charlotte's too hot to cuddle me
I hope all the time
I'll be her teddy for life.

Charlotte McDonnell (11)
St Anselm's Catholic School, Canterbury

HERNE BAY

Standing on my veranda
looking out at the sea

The strong north wind brushes
fiercely against my face
as I look down onto Herne Bay promenade

The sun is setting off the Isle of Sheppy
sinking into the horizon

There is a smell of freshness in
the air the sea front was silent
apart from the waves crashing
against the small pebbly stones

The place suddenly changed from
brightness to darkness and clouds
roar off the sea creating shadows

No longer is Herne Bay a place
you would want to see
winter has finally come.

Mark Jennings (14)
St Anselm's Catholic School, Canterbury

ROCKING DAYS ARE OVER

My favourite toy in all the world
Was a beautiful wooden horse.
I played with it all day long,
It never got tired,
Of course.

I loved my horse with all my heart,
Indeed he was a friend.
But now he's resting in our loft,
Next to the things that Dad needs to mend.

I used to pretend we were in lots of races
And we won them all.
I could only just get on him by myself
Because he was so tall.

And now he's resting in our loft.
No more can I pretend.
For I am much too big now
He was my very best wooden friend.

I was a lucky rocking horse,
I had a real good mate.
She played on me for so long,
That one day for playschool she was late.

And now I am locked up in the roof,
I am missing her a lot.
I am so very bored up here,
I wish that I could rock.

I think she was a very good rider,
Although she was only three.
For I was so tall,
And she was so small.
I knew and still do know that she loves me.

Nancy Johnson (11)
St Anselm's Catholic School, Canterbury

KNOWING

I stare out the window
Looking outside
Knowing what it is like
To have no future
To have no life
To know a disease
Is spreading inside
To feel the heartache
To feel the regrets
Not knowing what to do next
Does anyone care?
Is there anyone there?
Life is so unfair
Will anyone notice that I am gone
Their lives will just carry on
Each breath is becoming a struggle
I feel my last few breaths
Slipping away
Off I go
To somewhere
I do not know.

Louise Knight (14)
St Anselm's Catholic School, Canterbury

THE DARKNESS FILLS

The darkness fills
the open space
as the clouds conquer the sun
but still I am fearless
of what is yet to come

The gloomy grey mass
crashes so near
but now I see
I begin to fear
of the pain in
the devil's game

I tried to find a sanctuary
a place to hide
a place to find
the memories that I left behind.

Ben Jackson (14)
St Anselm's Catholic School, Canterbury

THE END

The bear I had was brown,
I liked him without a frown.
He never made me wail, scream or shout,
I liked him without a doubt.
I liked him because he was furry,
Friendly and full of joy,
I liked him the best,
So he was my favourite toy.

Did he feel the same about me,
Shall we ask and see.
'I liked him a lot, until he gave me away,
I did not want to depart,
I wanted to stay,
I wanted to play,
I did not want to go away.
He was my only real friend
Until he got rid of me,
That was the end.'

Samuel Brealey (11)
St Anselm's Catholic School, Canterbury

NOT ANOTHER DETENTION

It very first started in DT, I got a detention
For just being me.
All I did was chew some gum, answer back
And trip up someone.
My day got worse, because you see
My teacher just kept picking on me.
'Nicola you're in the wrong place.
Nicola please don't pull that face,'
The whole class turned to look at thee.
I wish the floor could swallow me.
The teacher *roared* 'Now class behave,
You're here to work, so face this way.'
I'm sitting here now all alone,
My detention nearly over, my freedom so close.
The teacher comes in and looks at me,
'You can go now' she said.
Hooray I'm free.

Nicola O'Sullivan (12)
St Anselm's Catholic School, Canterbury

How Would You Like It?

*(To Keiko the whale from Free Willy who like my whale
spent twenty-three years before he was freed again)*

I swam slowly through the water.
When I just felt a net over me.
'Mummy' I screamed but nobody heard.
I was taken to a small tank.
Just for three tiring movies.
Twenty-three years in captivity.
A lot of pain for a little pleasure.
Why can they not stop catching us?
I am now free after a lot of pain.

How would you like it?

Stephanie Cook (12)
St Anselm's Catholic School, Canterbury

The Dark Green Turtle

I'm swimming in the sea,
It's as green as it can be,
Some nets fall down and trap me,
Oh no oh no they've got me,
They start to pull me to the land,
I'm lying on my back in the sand,
Some men are tugging and pulling at me,
A boy ran out to reach for me,
He whispered in my ear,
Which got me over my fear,
I was soon let free,
We met in the morning at half past three,
And swam away together.

Rachel Child (12)
St Anselm's Catholic School, Canterbury

IT'S A GIRL

One day I found myself in a strange place
What am I doing here? Who am I? What am I? Why am I?
I started to wriggle and worm and kick and punch
Made my fingers into a bunch
And I could find that I could punch
I kept wriggling and wriggling
And itching and itching
Then all of a sudden
                    Pop!
Out came my head and I felt a force pushing me out
The first words I heard were
'It's a girl'
So that's what I am, I'm a girl
Waaaaaa!

Carlene Brendish (12)
St Anselm's Catholic School, Canterbury

MY SPECIAL BEAR

My big, brown bear is as sweet as can be.
I love him loads as you can see.
We've always been friends from the start,
Nothing could ever tear us apart.

We've been together since we were young.
We've been on some journeys and had a lot of fun.
We've travelled across the sea to Spain,
We went to France then home again.
I love that girl whose name is Claire,
I think that I'm a special bear.

Claire Ogilvie (11)
St Anselm's Catholic School, Canterbury

FLOPPSY!

Me: Ten year old teddy sitting on my bed,
          Big floppy green ears hanging off his oval shaped head!
          Big floppsy not Mopsy, Yes that's right!
          I cuddle him every night.
          He is a friend, a comforter, a soppy old thing.
          His old arms and legs are now a faded pale green.
          But still in my room this precious thing can be seen.

Teddy: Eleven year old girl dropping me on her bed!
          She's kinda short, blue eyes, brown hair, rounded head.
          She calls me *'Floppsy!'*
          Oh how I wish it was Mopsy!
          She pushes me out of bed every single night.
          Oh how it gives me a fright!
          She doesn't love me, cherish me, look after me
          No!
          Does she still love me? Oh it must be so!

Hannah Tutt (11)
St Anselm's Catholic School, Canterbury

HELLO WORLD

It's lovely and warm in here,
Dark soft and comfortable.
I've been here a long time,
And I'm starting to feel squashed!

Wait a minute! What's happening?
I can feel squeezing all around me.
I'm moving, sliding. I can hear noise.
I can feel cool air. I can see bright lights.

It's going fast now! What's happening?
My head's out - someone's pulling me!
Help - it's going too fast.

I've left my warm place
I'm outside now . . .
Who are all those people smiling at me?
And who's this holding me?
I've found another soft and warm place now!

Sophie O'Reilly (12)
St Anselm's Catholic School, Canterbury

THE OLD BARN

The old barn creeks in the wind like an old boat,
Creek.
The door rotten and worn out shows pathetic
attempts to patch up holes.
Creek.

Inside the barn the straw bed lies in the corner
Damp from last night's rain.
Creek.
The stone table has some scraps of food on it from
The last time the barn was used as a shelter.
Creek.
The cobwebs in the room are uncountable since it
Has not been cleaned for years.
I think I'll leave now for this place fills me with fear.
Creek.

Sam Quigley (12)
St Anselm's Catholic School, Canterbury

FREE FOR ME

Splashing, crashing,
Around in the sea.
Everyone shouting at me,
The nets crashed down I started to drown
My face was as red as a clown's nose,

Dragged, pulled to an unknown place,
Where was everyone's smiling faces?
We were going at a staggering pace.

The boat slowed down and I started to frown.
I heard a scream an almighty scream,
I couldn't understand,
I saw it, another *whale,* I was free.

Michael Holder (12)
St Anselm's Catholic School, Canterbury

THE BEACH

Sitting on the pebbles
On the beach one day
Watch the wave roaring
In going away.

The sun beating down on me.
I can see the seagulls
Flying around my head.

The sea breeze cool on my face.
Watching the boats and
The ships on the horizon.

Polly Ryan (14)
St Anselm's Catholic School, Canterbury

ALL I WANT IS TO BE FREE!

There I was swimming away
When a fisherman pulled me to the bay
I started to wave my arms and feet
But they didn't care because all they wanted was my meat.

This boy came pushing through the crowd
He had come to save me
That made me proud
Then he whispered in my ear.
Don't worry not to fear
I'm saving you, just one thing
I'm coming too.

On the bay we'll meet tonight
We'll sail together and see the sights.
Yes that's it we'll sail away
For a year, six months and a few days.
You won't be bothered ever again
So come with me don't take his pain.

All I want is to be free
Not to be used as meat.
Oh yes freedom at last
I want tonight to come so fast.

So there we were swimming away
For a year, six months and a few days.

Emma Markey (12)
St Anselm's Catholic School, Canterbury

MY BEAR EDWARD

I had a bear called Edward
a big brown bear,
with a big button nose
and big beady eyes

I had a bear called Edward
I climbed upon his head
I climbed upon his belly
and I climbed upon his leg

I had a bear called Edward
who was thrown down the stairs
his neck was broke and he did choke
because he lost the stuffing from his throat

I had a bear called Edward!

My owner's name is Michelle
her brother is a pest
they climbed all over me
and would not let me rest

They threw me down the stairs one day
my neck was broke so they put me away
and I am still there today.

Michelle Coast (11)
St Anselm's Catholic School, Canterbury

MY FRIEND ZIPPY

You've lost your looks
You're old and torn,
You have been with me
Since I was born.
Your name is Zippy
I don't know why,
You're who I look for
When I cry.
Now you sit
On my bed
With stuffing hanging
From your head.

She'd wrap me up
And hold me tight,
She'd keep me near her
Through the night.
She loved me
And I loved her
When she gave me a hug
I gave her a purr.
I know I'm not so pretty now
And that I'm getting old,
I've still got some life in me
And I do as I'm told.

Nicola Phillis (11)
St Anselm's Catholic School, Canterbury

ME AND MY TOY FRANKY

I have a soft toy hedgehog
His name is Franky
He used to be my favourite toy
He went everywhere with me

On her way back from France
On the ferry
Out of all the other toys
Of course, she chose me!

He wears tartan dungarees
A green bow tie and red shirt
His whiskers have been pulled out
And he needs to go on a diet

She used to throw me everywhere
And hug me round the neck
I'm sure she was trying to strangle me
And she drops me out of bed

I always used to talk to him
When I was sad or angry
Although he never answered
I was sure he had heard me

She spilt water all over me
And I got all soggy
I had a close encounter
With her hamster Harry

Now I am still here
He's sitting on my bed
She's my favourite person
And he's my favourite ted!

Stephanie Renn (11)
St Anselm's Catholic School, Canterbury

SORRY!

'When you threw me in that canal
I came out filthy wet and cold.'

'I didn't mean it Super Ted, I had only
just gone three years old.'

'We're your books up here on the shelf.
The ones you're never looking at.'

'OK you win, I lose, I, I . . .
Suppose you have a point with that'

'Hey it's me your jigsaw puzzle
I hear two of my pieces are out of town.'

'OK, OK, I'll admit to that, last week
I sold them to Timmie Brown.'

'Oi down here it's your old toy lorry
I'm missing two of my wheels!'

'I just, I just don't know what to say
I'm beginning to see how it feels.'

'Now you know how it must be,
for jigsaw, books, Ted and me the lorry.'

'I think I've learnt my lesson now,
I just want to say I'm *sorry!*'

Stevie Withington (12)
St Anselm's Catholic School, Canterbury

WINTER IN THE WOOD

In the wood in the warm hot summer
Things are just so much funnier
Then in the ice cold freezing winter
'Cos the frost bites you just like a splinter
White sheets of snow cover everywhere
And branches hang as bare as bare
As for the birds well they all go
To where it's warm and there's no snow
Other animals all hide
In their holes nice and warm inside
And I am in the place I hate
Under the ice-coated lake
But when the beautiful spring comes
I'm reunited with my chums
And I am happy every day
Until next winter comes and the sun goes away.

James Tee (12)
St Anselm's Catholic School, Canterbury

EYES OF A TEDDY

Good night James and God bless,
In the morning . . .
We could clean up our mess.

(annoyed)
Running here running there,
Where we go I don't care,
The swings or a funfair,
Where we go *I don't care.*

Shall we run down the stairs,
We could be lions . . .
Or possibly big hares.

(tired)
Running here running there,
Where we go I don't care,
The swings or a funfair,
Where we go I . . . don't . . . care.

Gregory Ross (11)
St Anselm's Catholic School, Canterbury

TED

I just moved into a new house.
Oh! How different this all felt
Until one day in the attic dark
There I found a toy mouse.
It was soft and cuddly and it
made me feel warm.
And I felt to take this mouse
in my pocket safe.
Until one day disaster struck
when out of my pocket it fell.
Down, the hill and over the glen
down the hole into the den.
Oh how different this den feels
where is my happy friend?
Life will never be the same again.
Now I am in this foreign land.

Kevin Murray (11)
St Anselm's Catholic School, Canterbury

MY TED

My favourite toy when I was four,
was my teddy named *Big*,
But he only has one claw,
And he wears a brown wig.

I hate that baby boy,
He hits me once *no* twice
He thinks I'm just a toy,
And he stuffs me with *rice!*

My ted has a plastic nose,
And he has black eyes,
He has a hanky as red as a rose,
And he is an almighty size.

I hate that baby boy,
He hits me once *no* twice,
He thinks I'm just a toy,
Because he fills me with *rice!*

My ted has brown fluffy fur,
But my dog took his arm,
I always call him sir,
But he did live on a farm.

James Bowyer (11)
St Anselm's Catholic School, Canterbury

PLAYSTATION POWER!

My PlayStation is my favourite toy,
It's grey with a light which shines with power,
A button which reveals the compartment for CDs,
It has a reset button which resets the computer
It has a wide range of games from racing to strategy,
Titles come from Wacky Worms to Gran Turismo and many others
The array of adaptations,
A shaky pad to a steering wheel,
A mouse to multi tap,
Memory cards and many others,
Which is why I think what does my PlayStation think of me . . .
My PlayStation would think of me as *God*,
I am the only one who uses it properly,
I never abuse it and I'm its friend,
Others call it stupid, addictive and a waste of money,
But I stand up for it whatever they say,
He would like me because I give him plenty of action,
I gave him a reason to live,
He would recognise himself as a hero and some back.

Matthew Wearing (11)
St Anselm's Catholic School, Canterbury

A Life

As a life ends, a day begins.
As summer starts, spring stops.
As the sun goes down,
The moon comes up.
As rain stops, rainbows shine.
Nothing comes at once.

There are no friends
Without hate.
No joy without pain.
Everything hits you at once.

No good is too bad.
No thought is too mad.
Along life's road,
There's many a corner,
Only one choice is for choosing.

Tom Mackay Miller (13)
St Anselm's Catholic School, Canterbury

Morning

I drew the curtains to feel a warm gentle light upon my face.
I saw the green green grass through these clouded eyes of mine.
The birds singing the morning chorus, rays of light bouncing off
the tranquil lakes, the people opening their doors to a new day and
breathing in the crisp morning air.
The ringing of a bell when the paperboy rides by,
and children being sent off to school.
People putting their washing out and chatting to their neighbour.
And so the day rolls on to the darkness of night, and so approaches
the morning which I dare not to fight.

James Kent (13)
St Mary's Westbrook School, Folkestone

THE OWL

The owl she floats and glides,
as the moon shines behind her
and reflects upon the water below,
The lake so quiet, shadowed and deep,
So haunting as mist across its surface creeps,
The owl ignores the mist ahead
and flies toward her nesting bed,
Then drops her prey upon the twigs,
and with her beak her baby digs,
Then as she watches and cleans the nest,
Her baby eats and then they rest.

Elizabeth Clark (14)
St Mary's Westbrook School, Folkestone

WEATHER

The weather can be cold,
The weather can be hot.

Snow is cold,
The sun is hot.

When it rains,
Everything stops,
Puddles form,
Water drops,
And then the sun comes out,
And everywhere is dry again.

Venetia Kortlang (14)
St Mary's Westbrook School, Folkestone

LIFE

It has always puzzled me
How I spend my life.
Will I have a wife in my life,
To what sort of job
Will I end with?
Maybe a high paid lawyer
Or a dustbin man.
A couch potato
Or a rocket scientist
Perhaps I'll land on Mars
Or sell chocolate bars.
It doesn't really matter
How I'll spend my life.
As long as I live it.

Simon Dorney (13)
St Mary's Westbrook School, Folkestone

MY GARDEN

The garden is a place to unwind and dream.
The air is clean and the breeze is fresh.
I look at the trees and all the colours at its best.
The fish grow day by day in the pond.
The bird table is home to lots of birds.
Squirrels cats and baby toads.
The garden is certainly the peacemaker.

Christopher Renicar (13)
St Mary's Westbrook School, Folkestone

What Life's Like In A Hamster Cage

It's dark outside
I stretch
I look around my world
Then this thing puts a tree in my bowl
I go and see it
I smell it
Then start to take it to my house
It was very big and heavy
I got it there
I eat it all up
That's my life in a hamster cage!

Rebecca Renicar (13)
St Mary's Westbrook School, Folkestone

Autumn

The rushing of the leaves passing my feet
The different colours flying by
The royal reds
The golden yellows
The dark murky browns
The dull oranges
The squelch of the wet leaves beneath
my feet from the rain last night.

Maria Sorge (13)
St Mary's Westbrook School, Folkestone

PRIMARY SCHOOL

Monday morning, what a mess!
Homework not done, teachers in stress.

Assembly time, I've lost my tie!
Tuck my shirt in as headmaster walks by.

Lessons now, I watch the clock.
Spellings, colouring, tick-tock, tick-tock.

Break! At last! I run out to play.
Football on the field, not on a rainy day.

There's only just time to eat my snack,
before we get called in to go back.

Playing in the sandpit, my only joy,
mix it with water then throw it at Troy!

Lunchtime already? Could it be so soon?
Let's see what mum's made, sandwiches, yoghurt, she forgot my spoon!

Playtime again! Life is great!
Until the whistle blows and you find you're late.

Story time next, I sit with the crowd.
You think things are fine, till you have to read aloud.

I pack up my books, my lunch box too.
It's the end of the day, no more school!

Say bye to teacher, 'No I won't run'
Out in the playground I see my mum!

Walking home, I talk about my day,
My friends, my teachers - there's too much to say!

It's silent at home, without the bell,
no putting your hand up, or 'I'm gonna tell'.

I'm sure I don't miss it, I mean who would?
To go back to Primary School, I wish I could.

Joanna Wassall (15)
St Mary's Westbrook School, Folkestone

EMOTIONS

The boy with the melancholy eyes
Showed anger and despair
As the teacher grabbed him by the ear.
'You're coming to my office,' he said.
The boy just thought silently to himself.

The boy muddled in his thoughts started
To cry.
The teacher showed no sympathy and said
It was all lies.

'I did not do anything, Sir. I'm not lying.'
The teacher ignored the boy who was
Desperately trying and said,
'You will go to the head tomorrow; there
You will face the consequences of your
Actions. The boy showed no reaction.

Carl Pieries (13)
St Mary's Westbrook School, Folkestone

NEW YORK CITY

Darkness in the streets darkness all around you.
There is a man looking at your every move.
As you walk as you talk as you stride as you glide,
Through the streets of New York.
Up above and below the streets of New York.
You walk into an alley,
And all that can be seen is dark, dark, darkness.
You feel a heated breath on the left side of your cheek.
You see a shadow of an eye glisten in the night.
A light appears as you turn the weary corner.
You are surrounded by tall tall buildings.
You walk two or three blocks,
As you find no way to escape the four walls of New York.
People watching you near and far as a white light appears to blind your
every sight.
A door opens, eyes shut tight, silence growls throughout your ears.
You awaken in the darkened night.
Water dripping throughout your face, as fright reunites with your soul.

Dreams Dreams
New York City.

Selven Sanjivi (14)
St Mary's Westbrook School, Folkestone

School Days

On a cold and frosty morning,
Just as day is dawning,
I put my nose on the cold glass,
And realise I was late for class!

I ran down the stairs for breakfast,
As usual; I was last . . .
I grabbed my toast, butter and jam,
And left with my brother Sam.

In the classroom we unpacked our bags,
Said 'hi' to the guys, quoting a few gags,
Our teacher arrived ten minutes late,
With a gift under his arm, signed for Kate.

At 4 o'clock the school bell rang,
'Hooray for home time!' we all sang,
Children were rushing to board the bus,
To go home to dinner of chips and huss.

James Callaghan (15)
St Mary's Westbrook School, Folkestone

I Wonder I Wonder

I wonder I wonder
I think of the thunder
I think of the rain
And I go insane.

I wonder I wonder
I think of the sun
And I think of the day
That has just begun.

Mary Wetzel (13)
St Mary's Westbrook School, Folkestone

HOMEWORK

Homework is such a boring chore.
Sitting thinking.
Writing page after page.
As if a day at school wasn't bad enough.
When we come home it is another hour or so at least
before we are free for the evening.
It is 6 o'clock and time for homework.
Maths, English, French and RE piling up with Geography.
Get out textbooks, pencils, workbooks and homework diaries.
The pencil that started life at 3 inches, now, because of the gnawing,
it is almost non-existent.
Then you see the pile of homework still to do.
You look at the clock, it is 7.30, time for TV - just one programme
wouldn't hurt, but then it is back to the long hard slog.
It could be a long night.
It is 10.00 and time for bed, finally finished. You snuggle down
for a good night's sleep and dream of a world that only you know.
With homework done you rest your weary head before *school*
in the morning.

Francesca Day (14)
St Mary's Westbrook School, Folkestone

THE SCHOOLBOY

My day is like the British weather
Bright in the morning,
Bleak during the day,
And beautiful at noon.

Ring! Ring! It's time to rise,
And face the beauty of the sunrise.
Down I go to greet my parents,
Brothers and sisters.

Then suddenly overcast it is,
With sadness and anguish,
As off to school we go
Oh! I find that low.

Children chanting to the same old tune
Under the watchful eye of the teacher
The boy in the corner begins to cry
But instead of comfort, it's mockery he gets.

The clouds have cleared
For the final bell has been rung.
Ring! Ring! It's time for home
Oh! Home, sweet home.

Ibrahim Shelleng (14)
St Mary's Westbrook School, Folkestone

My Itchy Thumb

Did you ever have a friend
who was a pain in the neck
He'd annoy you so much
that you'd end up a wreck.

You'd moan and you'd groan
and you'd scream to your mum
well I had a friend
he was my itchy thumb

He'd niggle and tickle
and always be there
you'd tell him to go
but he'd look back and stare

Maybe I could learn
to call him a chum
no way hosé
he's my itchy thumb

Then he'd stop and you'd look
but you're left all alone
he's not a friend
you can call on the phone

I haven't an itch
from my toe to my tum
I miss him, could kiss him,
come back itchy thumb.

Mary Tilling (14)
St Mary's Westbrook School, Folkestone

MY FEAR

Deep as the ocean
blue higher than the clouds.
Floating free as a bird I'm happy,
I smile. Seconds pass by but time
stands still. I hope it will last forever
but I know I am wrong.

The sky turns grey and clouds
form over, rain starts to fall,
I frown. Falling faster I can't
slow down. I hear sounds in my
ears but it's far, far away. It's my
greatest fear. It increases in volume
pulling me closer to it. The alarm
explodes.
I look at the clock, I frown and turn
away. It's *Monday.*

Adam Wardley (15)
St Mary's Westbrook School, Folkestone

I AM

I am the mournful crying in the night,
I am the shadow on the moon's pure light,
I am the darkness, creeping inside,
I am that from which young children hide.

I am the stalker, the hunter most foul,
I am the blackness surrounding you now,
I am the starry-eyed torrent of Hell,
I am the tolling - of your death knell.

Milo Hanrahan (13)
Simon Langton Boys' Grammar School

THE SUPERHERO

Yeah, you shout.
You shout it loud and proud,
Like someone whose dreams had all come true.
I suppose they had.
In an hour and a half
You accomplished everything you ever wished.
I just wasted time.
I wasted an hour and a half
To watch you succeed,
To forget about my life,
And think about yours.
And now you're nothing,
Until the sequel
Or until I rent the video
And watch your achievements
For the second time.
But why would I do that?
Why would I waste another
Hour and a half
When I have
More important things to do?

Mischa Pearlman (17)
Simon Langton Boys' Grammar School

COMMUTING

The whistle is blown,
Hurry, hurry, jump on!
The train is ready
To continue its song.

Clickety-clack, clickety-clack,
The train is rolling along the track.

The passengers settle
To read or sleep.
They take little notice
Of the cows and sheep,
The orchards, the quarries,
The factories, the mines,
Or the derelict houses
Which back onto the line.

Clickety-clack, clickety-clack,
The train is hurtling along the track.

Two hours have passed
The station is near.
People gather their cases,
Their books disappear.
They hustle and bustle
To be first off the train.
After a day at the office,
They'll be back again.

Click-et-ty cla-a-ck, click-et-ty cla-a-ck,
The wheels are screeching on the track.

Christopher Coppins (13)
Simon Langton Boys' Grammar School

THE PERFECT BOY

This is a poem about the perfect boy,
He's really handsome and his name is Roy,
He wears cool clothes and Kicker shoes,
He likes Bart Simpson and hates the news.

He's as clever as a doctor performing an op,
He's as bright as a multicoloured, luminous top.
He's as hot as a cooker, so the girls think,
But when they all chase, he goes bright pink.

He's as brave as a boxer entering the ring,
He's as rich as a pop star, Prime Minister or King,
He's as fast as a rocket off into the sky,
But he's always alone. I wonder why?

Philip Smith (12)
Simon Langton Boys' Grammar School

WAR POEM

Sky flashes,
Guns thunder,
Huge crash,
Minor blunder.

Planes soar,
Adrenaline rush,
Heart beats faster,
Losing touch.

Bomb falls,
Mighty roar,
That's it,
No more.

Jack Baker Lewis (13)
Simon Langton Boys' Grammar School

THIS IS THE TRAIN

This is the train on the super fast track
Whistling down to Paris and back
Super-sleek engine styled with panache
Into the tunnel and gone in a flash.

This is the steam train chugging for fun
Passengers chattering as the trip is begun
Up through the valley, steaming the line
White smoke a-trailing, the views are just fine.

This is the train that rattles and creaks
The journey's not far but it seems to take weeks
Trundling past farmland, stopping and starting
Seeing at stations the greeting and parting.

This is the goods train lumbering slow
Rumbling alone with its trucks in a row
Laden with limestone or parcels or coal
Endlessly straining to reach its goal.

This is the train as its engine is slowing
The station is here and its passengers are going
The platform is empty except for the guard
And this train is shunting back into the yard.

Ben McElroy (13)
Simon Langton Boys' Grammar School

A CHRISTMAS CAT

I adore Christmas.

New people to pick me up and caress me,
I choose particularly the ones that dislike cats the most,
the ones who sneeze,

Playing with the cracker bits, chasing them under the
table, in amongst the forest of legs.
By accident, I ladder tights of the legs that kick me,

Wrapping paper to pounce on,
To jump and bounce on
To rip and shred and make a mess of,

Soft new clothes to sleep on, drop my white hairs on,
To dribble on,
To wriggle on,

And when the meal is finished, I adore, best of all,
Left-over turkey.

James Carpenter (12)
Simon Langton Boys' Grammar School

MOUNTAIN FEVER
(With apologies to John Masefield)

I must go up to the hills again, to the paths that wind up high,
And all I ask is a pair of boots and a map to guide me by.
And the high peak and the deep gorge and the cow-bells calling;
And the wide sky and the chough's cry and the view enthralling.

I must go up to the hills again, for the sunrise over the snow
Is a dazzling view and a beautiful view that lights the world below.
And all I ask is a fine day without storm clouds looming,
And a tree's shade and a stream's splash and the gentians blooming.

I must go up to the hills again, to the lure of the unclimbed peak,
To the full pack and the sore back and the feet that ache all week.
And all I ask is a cool breeze with the mist ascending,
And a hot bath and a good meal at my journey's ending.

Tom Spencer (12)
Simon Langton Boys' Grammar School

CHRISTMAS

Shining baubles hanging from the trees,
Poor people in Africa, they don't have any of these.
Lights brilliantly lighting up the snow,
Hungry people in Somalia - their crops didn't grow.
Decorations shining, very bold and bright,
People cold and hungry on this very night.

Lovely Christmas dinner, yum, yum, yum!
Hungry people fighting over every little crumb.
People drinking their glasses of sherry,
People dying in the streets, no reason to be merry.
Children getting very excited, on Christmas Eve,
Parentless children with a right to grieve.

These people live everywhere.
Neglected without any care.
We could stop this if we banded together,
Stop this once and forever.

Oliver Warr (12)
Simon Langton Boys' Grammar School

ME

I'm six foot four,
Eyes of green,
Handsome to the core,
A sight to be seen.

I'm from a different mould,
Head of jet-black curls,
With a heart of gold
And such a hit with girls.

Always ready with a smile,
Oodles of charm,
Bags and bags of style,
And not a drop of smarm!

Nick Waldron (12)
Simon Langton Boys' Grammar School

ME

I'm as cute as a kitten,
I'm as lightweight as a bee,
I'm as cool as a cucumber,
I'm as tall as a tree.

I'm as clever as a computer,
I'm as bold as a beagle,
I'm as quick as a cheetah,
I'm as swift as an eagle.

I'm as handsome as a peacock,
I'm as bouncy as a yo-yo,
I'm as dangerous as a viper
This poem's finished like a do-do.

Edward Acteson (13)
Simon Langton Boys' Grammar School

IS THAT REALLY ME?

I looked at him,
Who could it be?
What on earth!
Is that really me?

I looked at my expression,
Cold as a winter's day.
Am I really that bad?
Do I look at people that way?

I looked into my eyes
As lifeless as can be,
So empty, so sterile,
That couldn't be me!

Am I really that bad?
So remote, so forlorn,
Sometimes I wonder,
Why was I born!

Jo Harman (13)
Simon Langton Boys' Grammar School

AN ANSWER TO E E CUMMINGS

I would rather:

Visit my loved ones,
Throw away my guns
Stroll in the park
Forget my woes
Forgive my foes.

Enjoy my life,
Nullify strife
Eliminate stress
Tidy up my mess -
The mess of my life,
And start again.

Reunite with friends,
Make amends.
Live life to the full,
Never be regretful -

Than kill in war,
Or be killed.
Maybe for nothing,
Maybe for something.
But still dead.

Owen Calvert (14)
Simon Langton Boys' Grammar School

THINK LIKE A BIRD

Their feathers are white
They soar in the sky
They are really quite high.
Their beaks are orange and
Their legs are black.
They fly around in a big pack.
They don't complain,
Because they are all the same.
They fly really fast
In and out of the clouds.
Come soaring down
And make you want to frown.
Their eyes are blue,
As thick as glue,
You couldn't catch them!

Richard Kerrigan (11)
Sutton Valence School

THE GHOST AND WOLF FIGHT

T he haunted clearing that was once a large forest,
H ome to a wolf that slips around late at night,
E ating the remains of a dead rabbit.

F erocious wolves that search for a fight
O ut of sight goes the angry wolf,
R aging with anger as he pounded through the night.
E ager to see his cubs in the north,
S eeing his prey coming towards him,
T here he stood as quiet as a mouse about to have his early dinner.

Hannah Chitty (11)
Sutton Valence School

THE CHASE

She runs freely in the wild windy woods,
Where gypsies walk with coats and hoods.
You'll feel like you're being watched by her sinister eyes,
If you're small, run for your lives!
She has such a mighty bound,
Her kind live in fear, but she's never been found.
She has a playful litter of cubs,
They live together in the wild shrubs.
You may see her but not for long,
You'll only see a flash, then she'll be gone.
She hears the horn's loud blow,
Quickly, it's the chase, time to go.
She feels her heart's loud pound,
Her scent's been found.
She knows the race is on,
Off to the den, they won't find her there, they've gone.
She stops outside it, ears alert and eyes awake,
Then the hounds pounce, her howl is the last she'll ever make.
The hounds run off to tell their master,
Oh what a mess, what a disaster.
She limps off to her den to lie,
There she rests ready to die.
Her fur is thick and a rusty colour,
Her cubs come out and wimper around their dead mother.

Rebecca Jones (11)
Sutton Valence School

HUBBLY BUBBLY CHAMPAGNE

Hubbly bubbly
Up to the top
Up it goes
Pop

Hubbly bubbly is nice to drink
But when it is up your nose
It will make you sneeze
It will make you cough and splutter
It will even make you wheeze

So when you have hubbly bubbly
See that it does not go up your nose.

Alastair Cox (11)
Sutton Valence School

AN AUTUMN POEM

The trees look splendid with their coppery tint,
The colder weather gives us a hint,
Of the short days of winter still to come,
As the noisy children play conkers for fun.
People pick chestnuts to roast on the fire,
But the watery sun doesn't rise much higher.
The rain is making the ground quite wet,
The badgers don't like it and stay in their sett.
Leaves fall, acorns too,
That gives squirrels lots to do.
Animals hibernate and food is stored,
For winter, so they don't get bored.

James Dobson (11)
Sutton Valence School

SCHOOL

The dropping sleepy heads,
The boredom-stricken faces,
I think I'd rather be
in a million other places.

The punishment of school,
First thing in the morning,
How can I stay awake
when I can't stop yawning.

Maybe I'll wake up,
By break time at eleven,
I think that's fair enough
when I've been up since seven.

Ah, I hear the word 'video',
A half an hour nap,
I know I won't miss much
I bet it's pretty boring.

Eight more important lessons,
I think I'll just get through,
Although come to think of it
there's a million things I'd rather do.

Steven Groom (15)
Sutton Valence School

THE PRICE HE PAID

'Faster, faster, the enemy's coming.'
Over they go, not looking back,
Not trusting themselves to keep going.
They know the routine, the pain and fear
Wishing away the harsh reality.
But the screaming is all they can hear.
The hands of time keep ticking around them,
But the tiring fear dulls the pain of time.

Wearily they run into the face of danger.
There is now only a few yards to go.
They can advance no more.
A machine gun is firing to and fro,
Shooting all those who dared.
Jones pipes up, 'I can get that gun.'
He goes over the top, not showing he's scared.
Gallantly and victoriously he carries back the deadly weapon.

At eighteen he is pretty feisty,
Yet we have to scream to him to run.
But the gun is much too heavy,
He is shot and killed.

'We won', the radio proudly announced, but
At what cost? Don't they realise what he lost?

Alexandra Pugh (15)
Sutton Valence School

THE BATTLEFIELD

How many times must we take to the field?
So worn and scarred from battles prior.
The wounds are there, blanketed in denial,
But unforgotten.
Once committed we forfeit our freedom,
We are bound until the end.

With fear prickling from us we wait
And look over to the other side,
To the massed figures looming on the horizon,
Distant but dominant.
There they linger, sipping their cups of courage.
They do not, like us, dread what is imminent.

The cry of the alarm!
A sound so shrill that it quivers blood.
We fling ourselves to our weapons
But we are too late.
The storm of bullets is upon us
And with all the might we can muster, we retaliate.

But wait, that sound we hear again,
Not wailing this time, but soft and becoming.
We shed our armour, soiled with haste
And walk away.
Numb to the murmurs that beckon us back,
The 40 minutes is up.

Katie Gornall (16)
Sutton Valence School

MEETING A SQUIRREL IN BOURNEMOUTH

There he goes,
up a tree,
round and round,
he makes me
quite dizzy.

Down he comes,
onto me,
then jumps onto
another tree.

Then he climbs,
higher than high,
into the sky,
where only bees
and birds fly.

His twitchy nose,
His fur and tail,
His claws and gnawing teeth
which open waiting nuts.

He gathers up nuts
all summer long,
and waits until
the days are gone.

It's getting dark,
It's getting near,
It's getting clear
that winter's here.

Andrew Carr (11)
Sutton Valence School

SEABED

Walk across the hot, wet sand.
I cannot find the shade.
Try to fan myself.
Where is everyone else?
I feel faint.
Have to find some shade.
I realise.
There is a cave right there.
I sprint to the cave.
It's all in slow motion.
I trip and fall.
And roll to the sea.
The cool, lush water.
Sweeps over my body.
Slowly, slowly drifting.
No sound, no sun.
The seagulls do not cry.
Goodbye wonderful world.
I slowly sink.
Down and down.
To the bottom of the dark seabed.

Olivia Hendrick (11)
Sutton Valence School

UNTITLED

Watch the sand swish and swell.
A large trail of piled up sand to the water.
Two beady eyes look through the sand.
A greasy head of a snake pops up and shakes.

Here he comes up from the deep.
Watch him swirl.
Watch him dive.
Back to the deep.

The serpent has spiky skin.
And vampire teeth as clear as clear.
He waits till the dead have fallen.
When they fall into his depth he hunts them down.
Then swallows them whole.
After his meal he fades away into the black water.

Barnaby Clarke (11)
Sutton Valence School

I WOULD LIKE TO PAINT THE NOISE OF FIREWORKS

I would like to paint the
noise of fireworks,
I would like to paint the
joy of the mother with her newborn babe,
I would like to paint the fear
of students in an exam,
I would like to paint the future,
But most of all
I would like to paint the
noise of fireworks.

Lisa Evans (14)
The Archbishop's School

THE ROAD

The road reaches and coils,
Like a long black snake,
And then suddenly it turns,
To be straight as a garden rake.
It sees cars by day,
It sees cars by night,
It sees the world in calm,
It sees the world in plight.
During the day,
The cars come fast,
Nobody wants to,
End up last.
At night cars slow,
Lights cutting through the night,
Reaching from all the cars,
Giant arms of beaming light.

Tom Planner (13)
The Archbishop's School

THE CLOCK

There's a clock that stands in the hallway,
Doesn't do much else,
Doesn't tell the time,
Doesn't make a single noise.
Dad got the mender in,
He said it was past its sell-by-date,
But I like it,
And if it was gone I'd miss it.

Frances Jackson (13)
The Archbishop's School

THE WEEPING WILLOW

It was a cold December afternoon,
I can remember it clearly,
The wind was howling,
The clouds were threatening.

My dog and I
Went walking
Through a dark, dense wood
Filled with gossiping trees;
Spreading secrets only they can hear
We came to a stream; all frozen over
Quiet and still.

The trees had silenced
They stood as regimental soldiers,
I looked down the line
As a general inspects his ranks,
I noticed a tree of disgrace.

His long stringy arms,
All tired and withered
Reaching out for water;
For water that had fallen into winter's icy grip.

His thirst shall be quenched
When spring comes around again,
When he can drink the cool clear water.

Lauren E Ralph (13)
The Archbishop's School

A FRIEND

What is a friend?
Some would say
A friend is someone you can trust
Someone who can keep your secrets
Others would say
A friend is someone who is fun
Someone who makes you laugh

What is a friend?
Some would say
A friend is someone who likes you for who you are
Someone who laughs at your jokes
Others would say
A friend is someone who is there for you
Someone who looks out for you

What is a friend?
To me a friend
Is someone who is all of these things.

Faye Gardiner (13)
The Archbishop's School

THE BASEMENT

You never know what's in your basement,
It could be fat or thin,
It could have no hair or ears,
It maybe pretty dim!

It could have tiny beady eyes,
And a tinsy little nose,
With extra large yellow teeth,
With big and smelly toes!

Down in the basement late at night,
I creep and crawl so quiet,
I see a little rat run fast,
And cause a great big riot!

I thought I saw the basement hell,
I think I may be mad,
I slowly turn and look around,
And there I see my dad!

Danielle Mearns (13)
The Archbishop's School

THE GIANT SQUID

It lives near the largest part of the ocean,
It creeps through the water in a slithering motion.
Clammy suckers cling to innocent prey!
Whilst the crabs and the lobsters all scatter away.
Voraciously opens a sharp, beady eye,
Watching potential victims pass by.
Its flair to be able to shoot through the sea,
Is essential in times of great need.

Sharks risk their lives near this beauty unknown,
But as they come closer it seems to have grown.
It speeds to the surface to discover the earth,
It sees the new world like a baby at birth.
A fisherman spies it - he stops and he waits,
Can he tempt it with a morsel of fresh, smelling bait?
But who is the victim - most feared in the sea?
'No one' it says, 'will ever understand me.'

Bethany Bingham (13)
The Archbishop's School

HEDGEHOGS

A baby hedgehog is 1 day old
It's white and very minute
Even though it's very cold
It's very strong and cute.

As the hedgehog gets older day by day
They keep their nest quite hot
As the cold winter is on its way
The family makes room for one more lot.

The hedgehog takes a trip to the road
Not knowing where he is
As a lorry comes by with a heavy load
Beware little hedgehog cars go whiz!

Spike the tiny hedgehog
With a home that's made of logs
With spines as sharp as needles
Splat! He's just got squashed.

All his family comes and looks at him
And tears appear in their eyes
As he's lying there on the turf
Everyone says goodbye.

Jo Smith (13)
The Archbishop's School

GOODNIGHT

The day is done and the darkness
falls like a sheet of paper
carelessly tossed into the air.

I see the lights from a faraway
village dimming when the tired eyes
of the people close for night.

The black, clear sky is filled with
a glow as twinkling stars light up
the cool dark sheet above.

The day has ended and so must I
fall asleep for another day,
so goodnight and farewell - I close my eyes.

Felicity Clifford (14)
The Archbishop's School

BULLYING

Bullying, bullying,
In every corner of the playground.
Punching, kicking,
Name calling all around.
Physical and mental,
   Running home in fear.

If you're tall, fat,
   Small or black,
You get it just for being you.

They'll tease you on the bus,
They'll wait for you on the way home,
   And beat you up in the playground,
   And next day on the way to school.

If you wear glasses they call you four eyes,
Or if you wear a brace they call you metal
   Mouth.

You get it for anything at all,
   Just for being you.

Charlotte Savage (13)
The Archbishop's School

RUNNING FREE

Hooves make the snow crackle
As they gallop along having fun
Bucking, rearing wanting to play
Gleaming coats reflect the sun.

Running for miles, playing games
The snow is cold but they don't care
They don't want the day to end
Enjoying the fresh crisp air.

The day has turned to night again
They sleep dreaming under the holly tree
They dream of running in the snow
Running again, running free.

Emily Hobbs (13)
The Archbishop's School

LONELINESS

I sit lonely in my room,
All my thoughts are doom and gloom,
I wish better for myself,
But it never seems to come true.

I sit and cry all night and day,
But the loneliness never goes away,
I wish that I was someone else,
That's silly cos I am myself.

Oh why is it I am here today?
I wish I was far, far away,
Somewhere safe where I can stay,
Somewhere warm where I can play.

Natalie Powling (14)
The Archbishop's School

AUTUMN

Autumn is coming
Leaves are falling
Bonfires are smoking
You can smell them in the air

Autumn is coming
The trees look bare
The floor around them covered with
Brown and yellow leaves

Autumn is coming
The mornings are misty
The grass is wet with dew
It dries in the sun

Autumn is coming
Flowers are dying
No more holidays
Back to school

Autumn is coming
Daddy-long-legs are about
Spiders come in for shelter
Lights attract the moths

Autumn is coming
Football's just begun
Cricket's nearly over
The Ashes have just been won.

Neil Wade (13)
The Archbishop's School

RAINBOW

It looks as if somebody has reached up
high and painted a rainbow in the sky.

It's like a watercolour picture high
up in the clouds.
When a rainbow is in the sky people look
up and admire the rainbow.
Why does no one admire the plain blue sky?

The rainbow fades at the ends it is
getting ready to go.
Will the blue sky ever go?
No!
So next time you look up at the clouds
don't forget the blue sky and only admire
the rainbow.
Red
Orange
Yellow
Green
Blue
Indigo
Violet.
These colours make the rainbow, just don't forget!
But the blue sky is always there, so when a
rainbow appears look at that as well.

Emma Kennett (14)
The Archbishop's School

STORMY WEATHER

Early one morning
As me and my dog went out walking
I looked up at the peaceful clouds
Moving swiftly above the crowds
As if suspended by a long piece of string.

The peaceful clouds that once were
Above my head, have now turned to red
The crowds that were once there have gone
And that piece of string has got longer
Getting closer to the ground.

The red clouds now above my head
Start turning into shades of purple and black
People all around starting turning and running back
For they know that there is a storm about
And many people will scream and shout.

With a flash of lightning
The telephone mast starts brightening
With a gust of wind
The fences start to bend
And many people will scream and shout.

For today there has been stormy weather
With a flash and bang
And a gust of wind it all ends
And the sun lends itself back to the town
And the local people start to come back out.

Simon Luckin (15)
The Archbishop's School

THE GREY GREAT WHITE SHARK

The grey Great White which roams the ocean,
Moves quickly with a threatening motion.
Slowly at first, as it hears its prey,
The thrashing of legs on a warm summer day.
Children make noise as they innocently play.
Suddenly a fin rises through the ocean,
Parents run to get their son or daughter.
The shark glides swiftly away,
And doesn't come back at all that day.
After ruining the children's fun,
The shark disappears as quickly as it had come.
Maybe the shark had meant no harm,
Had not meant to disturb the calm.

Toni Latham (14)
The Archbishop's School

THE FIRE

You see this light
burning brightly
not knowing what it is
scaring you of what you will see.
You see it spreading
hurting you more and more
every second that you see.
The flame is more and more
as time goes on.
The fire goes further
not knowing of what to do
you run out of fear.

Maria Antoniou (14)
The Archbishop's School

MY GREAT TEACHERS

The first 18 years of life are spent,
Reading, writing and learning too.
Many teachers try their level best,
    To teach everything to you.

Only when you reach the end of it all,
    Do you really begin to appreciate,
The hard work, and time they took,
Even when you handed work in late.

I regret I did not work harder,
I did not do all the work they set.
All the knowledge I have thanks to them,
And the GCSEs they all helped me get.

Now I'm growing up,
There's still learning to be done.
My teacher's have done a good job,
    I thank them, every one.

Andrew Brown (16)
The Skinners' School

RONEN'S BREW

Neck of giraffe and,
Wart of toad,
Sting of jellyfish and,
Squashed hedgehog from the road,
Poisoned rabbits ear and,
Tail of a dead worm,
Eyeball of lion and,
5 dead rats go into my steaming brew,
All to make up Ronen's wonderful stew.

Ronen Buchalter (11)
Tunbridge Wells Grammar School For Boys

NASTY '98!

Rotten apple, T-bone steak
Throw these in, boil and bake
Myxomatosis, rabbit's ear
Chewing gum off Hastings' pier

All these things we stir around
To make our potion sure and sound

Sticky cowpat, slippery oil
Turn the rings on, make them boil
Infant teacher's torn out hair
Blue mould from some Camembert

All these things we stir around
To make our potion sure and sound

Rusty tap, dad's old sock
Dunk them in and set the clock
Schoolboy's gooey handkerchief
Genetically engineered sweetcorn leaf

All these things we stir around
To make our potion sure and sound.

Charles Jenkins (11)
Tunbridge Wells Grammar School For Boys

SUNLIGHT

A soft warming breeze
A shining sunbeam on trees
Sparkling on the lake.

Christopher Golland (11)
Tunbridge Wells Grammar School For Boys

FEAR

It used to be medicine
When I was young
A visit to the doctors was always fun
But now I'm older
It's not quite the same
Antibiotics are now the name of the game
Large red and white capsules
I'm expected to take
The first in the morning when I awake
They're the size of torpedoes
I'll never understand
Take with water, enough for a dam
15 capsules the bottle contains
I so look forward to no remains
The last of my five days is drawing near
That to me is the end of
My fear!

Robert Burton (12)
Tunbridge Wells Grammar School For Boys

FIREWORKS

Fireworks loud and bright,
All that noise is a fright.
All the colours, red, blue and green,
It really is a magical scene.

Catherine Wheels all alight,
It is a wonderful sight.
Children with sparklers running around,
A bonfire which gives heat and no sound.

Grant Sykes (11)
Tunbridge Wells Grammar School For Boys

THE SMELLY POTION

The powdered ear bones of a mouse
The mouldy green thing in the fridge of a house
A squashed speck of dust found on a road
And a quartered tongue of a flying toad
Half a wheel of a rollercoaster
And some small mechanics from a toaster
The halved stomach of a snake
A kilo of water from a mountain lake
And the year old edges of an old fish cake
A bit of thread from a bed
A bone of fish off a dish
And an extra large bump from an iron age lump
A year old antenna of a slug
And a red and yellow spotted bug.

Edward Jenkins (11)
Tunbridge Wells Grammar School For Boys

FEAR

I'm afraid of things in the night,
Things that might give me a fright.
The creaky old stairs, whistling wind,
I hope there isn't a spider lurking in the corner
ready to bite.
I'm afraid to be alone at night,
Watching the X-Files it scares me alright.
I don't like going up high,
I get the feeling I'm doing to die.
I don't like flying, it's the taking off I hate,
It's even worse if the plane is late.

Tom Goozee (12)
Tunbridge Wells Grammar School For Boys

SPIDERS!

I hate spiders! they make my skin crawl,
Just seeing them dangling on my bedroom wall,
I try to avoid them, at all costs,
But if one escapes I am lost.
I try to kill them, usually to no avail,
I try to squash them with a bathroom scale!
My mum tries to save them, and I don't really mind,
As long as she throws them out the window
Or somewhere else outside!
Some people don't understand my phobia,
And I suppose neither do I,
But it's not my fault
It's not my way
And it's *very annoying!*

Simon Griffiths (12)
Tunbridge Wells Grammar School For Boys

THE DEADLY STEW

Put into this pot of gunk all these things lump by lump.
Mickey Mouse's nose, toe of a slug, a piece of mum's best rug,
dirty football socks, an ancient grandfather clock.
Daffy's beak, homework written up in neat,
a paper bag and a cloth rag.
Mix it, mix it till it blows, uh oh there it goes down the street
in Mrs Brown's back door and scared her child with a roar,
freaked her out before chasing her out of the porch
and she was moving much faster than a walk.
So then she ran away across the land never to return
but then again the gunk never came back again either.

Thomas Daniel (11)
Tunbridge Wells Grammar School For Boys

A WITCH'S RECIPE

Heart of human,
newt too,
makes a lovely mix for you.
A drop of toxic chemicals fresh,
frog's spawn of a well past dawn.
Eight spiders legs,
a tongue of dog,
really does the job.
A rat's head,
plus a piece of decaying bread.
A red hot chilli,
an onion's spice.
A bat's wing
and a cat's tail
and a delicious rotting snail.
A Teletubby or two makes a bubbling stew.
A sting of bee,
makes a delicious recipe.

Morgan Grylls (11)
Tunbridge Wells Grammar School For Boys

I WISH I WAS A MILLIONAIRE

I wish I was a millionaire,
And go out every night,
But I wouldn't spend all my cash,
It just wouldn't be right.

I wish I was a millionaire,
And pay off all my debts,
But money doesn't buy happiness,
So I'd spend it all on bets!

Tom Langston (11)
Tunbridge Wells Grammar School For Boys

FEAR

Sharks.
In the sea swimming,
In the dark sea.
People wading unknowingly
With the sharks floundering free.
If you see one be sure to run,
Shark attacks aren't generally fun.
Some sharks are as fast as a horse,
While your skin is smooth,
A sharks is deadly coarse.
Their teeth can cut through bone,
Which will stop you from going home.
Sharks in the sea swimming,
In the dark sea.

James Miller (12)
Tunbridge Wells Grammar School For Boys

I WISH I . . .

I wish I could fly like a bird,
I wish I had magic Merlin powers,
I wish I was a millionaire,
Wish, wish, wish.

Sometimes I wish I were invisible,
Before I forget.

I wish I had no homework
And a three day weekend.

Simon Millington (11)
Tunbridge Wells Grammar School For Boys

SECRET POTION

Eye from a tiger,
Piece of a leaf,
Slime from a slug,
Money from a thief,
Mix it all together,
What do you get?
An old secret potion,
And don't you forget.

Hair from a doll,
Venom from a snake,
Finger from a boy,
Water from a lake,
Mix it all together,
What do you get?
An old secret potion,
And don't you forget.

Skin from a frog,
Tail from a dog,
A wing from a fly,
The end of a tie,
Mix it all together,
What do you get?
An old secret potion,
And don't you forget.

Simon Handley (11)
Tunbridge Wells Grammar School For Boys

WITCHES '98

Into the saucepan throw,
Watch the mixture swirl and blow!

Dr Pepper, throw it in,
With the beans from the bin.
Add the bowl of carrot soup,
And see the garden flowers droop.

Into the saucepan throw,
Watch the mixture swirl and blow!

Now in with the text books from our school,
And the bowl of doggies' drool.
Heat it with a drop of scotch,
And time it with a Rolex watch.

Into the saucepan throw,
Watch the mixture swirl and blow!

When the watch starts to chime,
Add a hint of lemon and lime,
Exhaust fumes give a colour bold,
And shelter us from the cold.

Into the saucepan throw,
Watch the mixture swirl and blow!

Chuck in the rotten egg,
And a single frog's leg.
Now the brew is done,
Put in the spoon and turn.

Into the saucepan throw,
Watch the mixture swirl and blow!

Calvin Davis (12)
Tunbridge Wells Grammar School For Boys

20TH CENTURY WITCH'S BREW

Plaque from a decayed tooth,
A pig's muddy hoof.
Nerve from a dog's brain,
The head of a child crying out in pain.
Stir it with a giraffe's neck,
And drink it, what the heck.

Waste from a nearby power plant,
Tiffany's husband Grant.
Genetically modified beetroot,
Neil Armstrong's space boot.
Stir it with a giraffe's neck,
And drink it, what the heck.

Eye of a cloned newt,
Bill Clinton's best suit.
John Major's speech,
Mould off a peach.
Stir it with a giraffe's neck,
And drink it, what the heck.

Kailan D'Arcy (11)
Tunbridge Wells Grammar School For Boys

ALLITERATIVE POEM

Four fantastic football players,
Fight for the ball, which is flowing fast.
Triumphantly Tim gets it, Tom tackles him tiringly.
Tim tussles with Tom.
Tim scores! Two-nil to the blue team.
Fans flood the field of fame!

Jack Nicholson (12)
Tunbridge Wells Grammar School For Boys

I AM AFRAID OF DYING

I have a fear, I'm sure most of you have,
It is the thought of dying.
Leaving everybody and everything behind,
My family and my friends.
It is also the thought of how sad
I would make them feel and
How I'd miss them so much.

I wouldn't be able to hug my parents
Or kiss them goodnight any more.
I wouldn't be able to grow up with them
Or live my life around them.

The biggest of my fears is
That I wouldn't forgive myself for
Not being able to say goodbye.
So now I see that the real fear is not of dying
But of leaving my family behind.

Greg Jones (12)
Tunbridge Wells Grammar School For Boys

FISH

An orange, rusty and black fish
With longish fins on the back
How quick it swims over and over
With a bluey, blacky smaller fish
With lots of blue fins all over
So slow and gracefully it swims
Not darting around like the other
How different they are.

Chris Knight (11)
Tunbridge Wells Grammar School For Boys

WHAT IS FEAR?

A great dark hole with an everlasting end.
A big hairy monster that growls under the bed.
A ferocious dog with a set of gleaming teeth,
or maybe a graveyard with ghosts of disbelief.

It could be a thriller,
or a late night show,
walking under a ladder,
or seeing a crow.

You might hate the water,
or being alone,
ever thought of a clone?
What is fear?

Daniel Meakins (12)
Tunbridge Wells Grammar School For Boys

WITCH'S BREW

Hubble bubble toil and trouble
oven heating, saucepan bubble

Eye of bat
and whisker of cat
Tongue of frog
and spine of a hog
Mix this round with the arm of a man
and add his hand as fast as you can

This is my magic witch's brew
with this you can do whatever you want to do.

William Hunnam (11)
Tunbridge Wells Grammar School For Boys

WITCH'S BREW 2001

Into the saucepan throw,
Cyber pets' egg and a yo-yo's yo.
Stripe of tiger, rhino's horn,
A blade of grass from a fresh cut lawn.

Rust of sword a thousand years old,
A devil's stone that's made of gold.
A lion's roar, a mouse's squeak,
A toe of a frog that's been dead a week.

Grain of sand, computer chip,
Cat's tongue and dog's lip.
Cola can and laser beam,
Darkness sucked from a nightmare dream.

Cobwebs and websites,
E-mails and alien frights.
Wing of bat, snakes slither,
Sheep heart and pig's liver.

Teletext, satellite dish,
CD-ROM and a witch's kiss.
Polluted water and river scum,
Stir it up, let's have some fun.

Triple, triple water spit,
Fire burn and flames lick.
Bubbles burst and stink rise,
Take a sip and say goodbye!

Max Ward (11)
Tunbridge Wells Grammar School For Boys

FEAR!

Mummy please don't leave me,
I'm scared all alone,
Please can you stay home,
Don't be silly dear,
The dog is in the kitchen,
He will keep you safe,
But, but, but . . .
See you in three hours, don't stay up too late.

I'm all alone, TV's the only light,
Something moves,
'Hello' I say, 'is that you boy?'
It is, I'm safe,
I slowly fall asleep next to him,
Cuddling up close, safe I hope!

About an hour later I was woken by a bark,
A loud menacing bark,
Now I'm very alert,
I look out the window,
Something's out there, I'm starting to scare,
My dog backs up whimpering and whining,
Something's out to get me,
Something very, very scary!
Crash! Something's in!
I hear heavy breathing, oh no . . .

I stay very still as it creeps around the corner,
I hear a growl, a bare of white teeth,
Sharp white teeth!
It jumped on top of me,
I'm dead meat!
Ahhhh, I woke up screaming,
I must have been dreaming,
Or was I?

Karl Gebbie (12)
Tunbridge Wells Grammar School For Boys

FEAR

I'm afraid of hairy spiders,
heights, jellyfish and baby minders.

First they crawl around and around
Making my heart pound and pound.
Up and down the wall they go
While I scream until they go!

Jellyfish are my next fear,
I've never actually been that near.
With their extra long tentacles
They'll reach me from Brighton to Dorset coves!

When I'm up high
I could swear I'm doing to die.
Up above the world I am,
If I fall off I'll end up like jam!

Baby minders are so kind
Until they start to blow your mind.
They send you to bed ignoring your cries
And when Mum comes back they tell her lies!

Laurie Beard (12)
Tunbridge Wells Grammar School For Boys

WHATEVER YOU LIKE 98!

Glasses of Elton John,
A Nintendo game that's been out long,
Frock worn by Mel B,
A drop of water from the sea,
Ears of Tony Blair,
And a strand of his hair.

Hubble, bubble, toil and trouble,
Some people moan and some people grumble.

Mad dogs' hair, cap of warden,
Eye of a Siamese twin,
Copies of books never written,
Dead gas man's nose,
And bills overdue from far and near,
Mix it up and stir it in.

Hubble, bubble, toil and trouble,
Some people moan and some people grumble.

The worst homework,
School dinners too,
Dead man's toes,
And the loo,
A teacher's head,
Pupils too,
Horse chewed grass,
And a cowpat toe.

Mix it all together and what have you got?
A liquid that's very hot.
Cool it with a monkey's blood,
Then add a pound of mud.

Joseph Farthing (11)
Tunbridge Wells Grammar School For Boys

FEAR

Fear of something lurking around in the dark upstairs,
Quickly I crept round each corner turning a light on.
Looking under the bed,
Inside the wardrobe,
Behind the door,
In the bath,
And in the attic.
Hang on a minute, I just heard something move.
Shhh!
Down the ground I crawl round the last corner and check the last room,
I look round in the dark and couldn't hear or see anything.
Suddenly I hit the light switch and checked;
Behind the computer,
In the wardrobe,
Wait, the other wardrobe door's opening.
I looked and realised someone had played a trick on me.
It was an inflatable waterbed blowing up and opening the door.

Tom Rainbow (12)
Tunbridge Wells Grammar School For Boys

AT SCOUTS

I was crouched down
They could not see me
I was covered in black from head to foot
They still didn't see me
They left, everything was still and quiet
The trees were still and it was a cold winter's night
The winter's wind brushed against my face
It was a freezing blast
My partner tapped me on the back
And said 'Let's go.'

Joe Middleton (11)
Tunbridge Wells Grammar School For Boys

FEAR

Fear, fear, fear.
Sometimes I think I hear,
Strange noises from my bedroom.
But when I go to see,
It's just my mind playing tricks on me!

Snakes are *sometimes* nice,
But you never know when they might attack!
The thought of them wrapping themselves around you,
Makes me shiver and scared at night!

Heights are totally daring,
And also quite suspending.
But if you look down,
Staring stiff at the ground,
You won't be hanging around for much longer!

Some men say,
'Courage faces fear and thereby masters it.'
And others say,
'Cowards repress fear and they are mastered by it.'

Tom Brown (12)
Tunbridge Wells Grammar School For Boys

SAND

Sand, sand is everywhere,
Between your toes and in your hair,
Wherever you look,
Wherever you stare,
You can be sure sand will be there.

Adam Reavely (11)
Tunbridge Wells Grammar School For Boys

Fear

I walk into a dark area of wood
and look all around.
Noises all around me and there is no
way out.
I run in desperate hope to escape.
The leaves underfoot crackle.
An animal is in the bush watching
your every move.
The trees tower above you
as if they're an adult.
I am at the superior mercy of nature,
begging it to let me out of its grasp.
I eventually escape leaving the haunting
noises and tall dark trees behind.

Daniel Boulton (13)
Tunbridge Wells Grammar School For Boys

Fear Of Fire

I'm afraid of fire,
The big red flames beckoning me in,
The overwhelming instinct to hurl myself in,
The warmth of the flames singeing my eyebrows,
The red embers glowing away in oblivion,
The light of the flames blinding my eyes,
Sensing pain and burning,
The fear of self combustion,
The sense of death,
The wild instinct taking over,
Self control fading, fading, fading . . .

Christopher Wilford (12)
Tunbridge Wells Grammar School For Boys

FIREWORKS

Smoking dry wood engulfed in flames,
whistles, bangs in the distance, tremendous
explosions with colour bursts, sparklers whiz
through air, Catherine wheels full of life.
Crackerjacks bouncing into the sky in a blitz
of air bombs and rockets.
Flashing thunder rockets, the best and most
expensive ones explode from the pitch-black
sky like a meteor destruction, fountains and
mine eruptions everywhere, the world gone up
in a fireball.
At last all is finished, died away, still bangs in
the distance echo off surrounding buildings.
Nothing left but ashes and cinders and
blackened out cardboard packages strewn
everywhere.

Chris Garner (11)
Tunbridge Wells Grammar School For Boys

FEAR

I'm scared of the dark
But I don't know why.
It's rather childish
But so am I.

I feel as if I'm different
Just because I'm scared.
I know it's rather silly
I wish I wasn't scared.

Robert Worsley (12)
Tunbridge Wells Grammar School For Boys

TRAIN RIDE

Swifter than eagles, stronger than bears,
We don't know where we're going
But really who cares?
Faster than a bullet coming out of a gun,
Faster and faster than Formula One.
Going past meadows, birds in trees,
Going past brambles and a hive full of bees.
Going over hills, passing through tunnels,
Coal in the fire and smoke out the funnels.
Passing windmills, passing flowers,
Passing fields, houses and towers.
Passing through Lingfield, passing through Reading,
Passing a church just starting a wedding.
Slowing down, stopping at a station,
I don't understand, I can't work this equation.
It's time to get up and off the train,
But still I'll be back tomorrow again.

Lawrence Nugent (11)
Tunbridge Wells Grammar School For Boys

FOOTBALL

F ootball is very enjoyable, I love it.
O wn goals don't happen very often.
O llay! Ollay! Ollay! Shouts the crowd.
T wo-one up and ten minutes left.
B all coming towards our goal.
A nxiously waiting for the next thing to happen.
L anky goalie who can reach the bar.
L et's have a shot thought number 9 - it's saved.

Luke Howell (11)
Tunbridge Wells Grammar School For Boys

FEAR

I fear claustrophobia,
Small spaces, tight spaces,
Lifts aren't bad,
But small, confined spaces,
Definitely not!

I fear going upstairs without any lights on,
I'm afraid something might jump out of the dark!
The dark can be scary,
But only if you imagine it is.
But if you stick up for yourself and walk straight upstairs,
Not looking into the dark spaces,
You will never fear the dark again.

Martin Leeder (12)
Tunbridge Wells Grammar School For Boys

GUESS WHAT I AM?

I have two hands and a face.
My hands move, but I cannot hold anything.
People look at me but I cannot see them.
Sometimes I have feet but I cannot walk.
I am sometimes made from wood.
I am reliable, but I need to be looked after.
I cannot hear, but when I speak, people listen.
I can get wound up, but I do not lose my cool.
Your time starts now.
What am I?

William Oakley (12)
Tunbridge Wells Grammar School For Boys

FEAR

I am scared of swimming in the sea
Are there creatures beneath me?

I am very scared of heights
Especially when I'm in planes at night.

Those gruesome spiders they scare me
They are always in the bathroom when they shouldn't be.

I hate it when I am in lifts alone
Going up and down and up and down it makes me groan.

Last of all I hate bees
Flying around they bother me.

Sam Batchelor (12)
Tunbridge Wells Grammar School For Boys

FEAR

What is fear?

Does it go bump in the night
And give you a fright?
Or does its eyes follow you everywhere
With its deadly frozen glare?
Does it have strong thick skin
Unpiercable by the strongest pin?
Or a stealthy dark brain
From a creature that dwells in the drain?
Does it live in the shade
Undisturbed by the loud, busy parade?
Or is a figment of our imagination,
An excuse to scare our brothers?

Sam Andrews (12)
Tunbridge Wells Grammar School For Boys

INTO THE CAULDRON GOES . . .

A batch of chemical waste,
Disgustingly foul in taste.

A piece of rotting meat,
Boiling in the heat.

A stale corpse,
Dug up from his grave who's name is Dave.

A glass of foaming acid,
This cauldron better be massive.

A mixture of chemical fumes,
Prepare to meet your doom.

A collection of viruses and disease,
They will do the deathly deed.

A crushed skull,
Now the cauldron is full.

> The spell is now cast,
> Your life is in the past.

Lee Francis (11)
Tunbridge Wells Grammar School For Boys

WINTER'S DAY

It is a winter's day,
The sun, blue skies all brushed away,
The snow falls down from the sky,
Like sugar from the mighty high.

It is a winter's day,
Snow everywhere,
On rooftops like icing on a cake,
Kids go ice-skating on a frozen lake.

It is a winter's day,
Snowflakes on every window ledge
As they sparkle on the window.

It is a winter's day,
Today is winter,
Tomorrow maybe not,
For at this moment winter is not.

Gad Mimran (11)
Tunbridge Wells Grammar School For Boys

THE MOUNTAIN

I see a dark mountain,
Through the misty air,
It is a place of darkness,
Filled with despair,

> I see a dark mountain,
> The trees are tall and thin,
> The appearance of the mountain,
> Makes it tall and grim.

I see a dark mountain,
It is black 'n' white,
If you ever go there,
It is just a deathly quiet.

> I see a dark mountain,
> No one skis there,
> All the people I have seen,
> Have just said 'Beware!'

James Martin (12)
Tunbridge Wells Grammar School For Boys

MIXTURE FROM HELL

Spoon of coffee,
Throw in the toffee.
Pile of herbs,
Before the lemon curd.

Rust from steel,
Axle from wheel.
Hands from Big Ben,
Ink from a pen.

Couple of tyres,
Tangled up wires.
Next a computer chip,
Before a monkey's lip.

Next a tea bag,
A nasty fag.
A dollop of gel,
It's the mixture from hell.

Boil for an hour,
Ensure it's sour.
Let it bubble,
Then there'll be trouble.

Owen Hunnam (12)
Tunbridge Wells Grammar School For Boys

FEAR

A big hairy spider really scares me,
They crawl and scamper and then they flee.
Tarantulas are really hairy and scary,
All big spiders really scare me.

When a great big dog comes and barks at me,
I quickly run home to get my tea.
A massive Alsatian is so ambitious,
And a tiny Jack Russell is just as viscous.

Heights to me are really freaky,
Whenever I'm high, I feel peaky.
You couldn't pay me to bungee jump,
Because I'm scared, I'll land with a bump.

I'm scared that I will die horribly,
Without anyone warning me.
Death will eventually overcome my life,
And I'm scared that I won't even have a wife.

Chris Edwards (13)
Tunbridge Wells Grammar School For Boys

THE FOREST

The grass is green, strong and tall
Other parts are in a mall
The trees are high and sway far
But won't smash like a jar
When old and very weak
They will topple like a leek
Sometimes big, sometimes small
One day every tree shall fall.

James Jones (11)
Tunbridge Wells Grammar School For Boys

THE RACE!

When the lights went out
It was the start of the race
They left the start of the grid
At a very fast pace.

Down the straight to the first
Corner at a hell of a dash
Nine times out of ten there's a
Very big crash.

Down the straight towards the
Chicane for sixty laps there's
More of the same.

Halfway through it's time for
A stop, four new tyres, ten
Seconds on the clock.

Into gear for the second half
Of the race, pit boards say I'm
In first place.

If you catch a back marker
It's a bit of a drag
Not long now till the end
Of the race.

Across the line in record time I'm
In first place, it feels so fine to
Win a race, the pleasure's all mine.

Anthony Copper (13)
Tunbridge Wells Grammar School For Boys

FEAR

Spiders, spiders and things in the dark,
Coming to get you, tear you apart.

In your house you're all alone,
And then you hear a terrible groan.

It's just your house starting to creek,
Or was it your dog, but he's asleep.

Something moves in the house of fear,
Or is that the murderer coming near?

It's just your mum you silly thing,
She's just come back from where she's been.

She has only been busy upstairs,
But, oh well, who really cares?

Roger Comben (12)
Tunbridge Wells Grammar School For Boys

I WISH I WAS A PUSSYCAT

I wish I was a pussycat that sits at home all day.
I would sleep whenever I felt tired and never have homework to do.
Whenever I felt bored I would chase a fly around the house.
I'd purr when I wanted attention and miaow when I needed food.
My fur would be soft and warm and everyone would want to stroke me.
Oh I wish I was a pussycat that sits at home all day.

Mark McKie (11)
Tunbridge Wells Grammar School For Boys

THE LONE SOLDIER

Down in the dark woods
What do you hear?
I hear snapping noises of dead twigs,
And the dripping noises of the wet rain.

Down in the dark woods
What do you hear?
The noise of clinking metal,
And my heavy heartbeat.

Down in the dark woods
What do you see?
I see a bogeyman figure darting out of sight,
And a startled animal wondering what all the bother is about.

Down in the dark woods
What do you see?
I see unknown danger all around me.,
And little mice filled with panic darting to safety.

Down in the dark woods
What do you smell?
I smell the dampness of the ground that I walk on,
And the smoke of a gun.

Down in the dark woods
What do you smell?
I smell danger,
And even death.

Down in the dark woods
What do you feel?
A cold rifle aiming at my head,
And the dead leaves at my face.

Daniel Mayhook (11)
Tunbridge Wells Grammar School For Boys

SPRING

Blossom fills the picture.

Lambs jump round the painting,
and noises like a newborn chick, calling to its mother for food.

A new weather changes the picture.
Different noises add to the painting, and all the animals learn
to walk or fly.

The snow is gone from the picture.

The ice from the painting, and animals can come out of
hibernation once more.

Lewis Haldenby (11)
Tunbridge Wells Grammar School For Boys

FREDDIE, WHO READ SCARY BOOKS AND WAS EATEN BY A SHEEP!

Freddie Watts was small and wise,
But scary books, they made him cry;
His mum did try to sort him out,
The only way was to scream and shout,
Those dreadful books she collected up,
Were driven away in the dustbin truck.
He still had nightmares in his sleep,
And was eaten by an enormous *sheep!*

Lee Mills (11)
Tunbridge Wells Grammar School For Boys

FIRE

The people sleeping unaware,
That a tongue of flame,
Lurks out there.

The fire waiting,
To begin,
As it burns
It is only hating,
All that it consumes.

Fire, fire the lord of fate,
Burning coals fall over the grate
As the flame leaps and pries
All you can hear are shouts and cries,
Of the house falling down,
Tumbling downwards towards the ground . . .

Lewis Cox (12)
Tunbridge Wells Grammar School For Boys